The Atlas of
ISLAM

All enquiries should be addressed to:
Barron's Educational Series, Inc.
250 Wireless Boulevard
Hauppauge, NY 11788
http://www.barronseduc.com

Library of Congress cataloging-in-publication data is on file.
Library of Congress Catalog Card Number
2002108883

International Standard Book Number
0-7641-5631-4

The Atlas of Islam was created and produced by
McRae Books Srl, via de' Rustici, 5 – Florence (Italy)
info@mcraebooks.com
Publishers: Anne McRae, Marco Nardi
Text: Neil Morris
Illustrations: Paolo Bracci, Lorenzo Cecchi, Gian Paolo Faleschini, MM Illustrazione
(Manuela Cappon, Valeria Grimaldi), Antonella Pastorelli, Paola Ravaglia, Studio
Stalio (Alessandro Cantucci, Fabiano Fabbrucci, Andrea Morandi, Ivan Stalio)
Picture research: Leah Coffrey, Daniela Morini, Laura Ottina
Graphic Design: Marco Nardi
Editing: Joanna Buck, Laura Ottina
Layout and cutouts: Laura Ottina, Filippo Delle Monache
Color separations: Litocolor, Florence

Printed and bound in the Slovak Republic
by TBB
987654321

THE ATLAS OF
ISLAM

Neil Morris

Illustrations Manuela Cappon, Gian Paolo Faleschini, Studio Stalio
(Fabiano Fabbrucci, Alessandro Cantucci, Andrea Morandi, Ivan Stalio)

BARRON'S

Contents

Spiral arabesque mosaic from the dome of the Lutfallah Mosque in Isfahan, Iran. This is a wonderful example of Safavid tilework. It was completed in 1619 under the Safavid shah Abbas the Great, who moved his empire's capital to the city.

This Moroccan panel contains the words of the Islamic shahada, or "declaration of faith." The words are embroidered in gold thread in the shape of a person praying.

Prayer is an important part of Muslim worship. This 19th-century Mughal miniature shows a man praying.

The crescent moon was the emblem of the Ottoman Empire, appearing on military standards and the tops of minarets. It became a symbol for the Muslim world in general and appears with a star on the national flags of many Islamic countries. The crescent may be associated with the Muslim lunar calendar.

Left: The beautiful Court of the Myrtles in the Alhambra palace, Granada, Spain. This part of the palace was built for the Nasrid ruler Yusuf I (ruled 1333–54). The Nasrids, who were the last of the Muslim dynasties in Spain, controlled Granada for more than 250 years until it fell to the Christians in 1492. During that time the city's artists, scholars, scientists, and merchants made it a great cultural center.

This 15th-century illustration shows a Sufi (Muslim mystic) with all his belongings – an animal skin, a staff, and a begging bowl. In their search for a closer relationship with Allah, many Sufis in the past gave up their worldly goods and begged in order to live.

Introduction

This book explores the history and geography of one of the world's great religions, tracing its beliefs and customs as they spread across the globe. Islam began almost 1,400 years ago in what is now Saudi Arabia, when the Prophet Muhammad received revelations from Allah, the only God. The Arabic word *Islam* means "submission" and its followers, called Muslims, submit and devote their lives to the will of Allah. The early Muslims soon spread their beliefs beyond Arabia, as their religion became a way of life, guiding their entire culture and society. Many different dynasties of caliphs and other rulers reigned over Muslim empires across three continents from Baghdad to Cairo and Cordoba. Through the centuries they developed aspects of art, architecture, science, and technology that are still wonders to us today. Now more than a billion people follow the unifying faith of Islam, with more than three-quarters of them outside the Arab region.

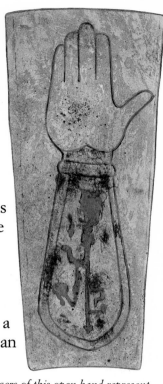

Mecca, where the prophet Muhammad was born, is the holiest city in the Islamic world. This miniature shows the city's Great Mosque and the Kaaba shrine, to which all Muslims turn when they pray.

The five fingers of this open hand represent the Five Pillars of Islam – basic duties for all Muslims. The hand appears on the keystone of an arched doorway of the Moorish Alhambra palace in Granada, Spain.

The prophet Ibrahim (Abraham), who is seen by Muslims as the first hanif, or "seeker after God." The great religions of Islam, Christianity, and Judaism all look back to Abraham, the patriarch who scholars believe lived soon after 2000 BCE. The three religions share other prophets, such as Moses (Musa), David (Dawud), and Solomon (Sulayman). Most importantly, they all believe in one all-knowing God, rather than the many gods and goddesses of other ancient peoples. They have very different beliefs about Jesus (Isa), however. To Muslims, Isa was an important human prophet.

Studying, reciting, and learning the Qur'an are very important to all Muslims. Children throughout the Islamic world are taught the Arabic alphabet. They can then learn how to pronounce the words of the Qur'an correctly. Many adults learn all the chapters of the holy book by heart. This boy is studying the Arabic alphabet in a Qur'anic school in Oman.

Medallion over a gateway arch in the Aqmar Mosque, Cairo, built in 1125 for the Fatimid dynasty. Inside is a repeated inscription of the name of Muhammad, and the very center of the medallion shows the name of Ali, the Prophet's cousin and the fourth caliph. The Fatimids were Shi'ites, and their caliphs claimed descent from Fatima, the Prophet's daughter, and her husband Ali. The Shi'ites, who take their name from the Arabic Shi'at Ali (meaning "party of Ali"), do not accept the first three Sunni caliphs and regard Ali as Muhammad's first true successor.

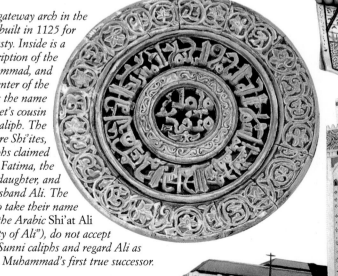

The King Hassan II Mosque in Casablanca, Morocco, was completed in 1993. Its 650-foot high minaret towers over the mosque, which also houses a Qur'anic school, library, and exhibition hall.

These Muslim children from Singapore are wearing special clothes to celebrate the Id al-Fitr festival at the end of the Ramadan fast.

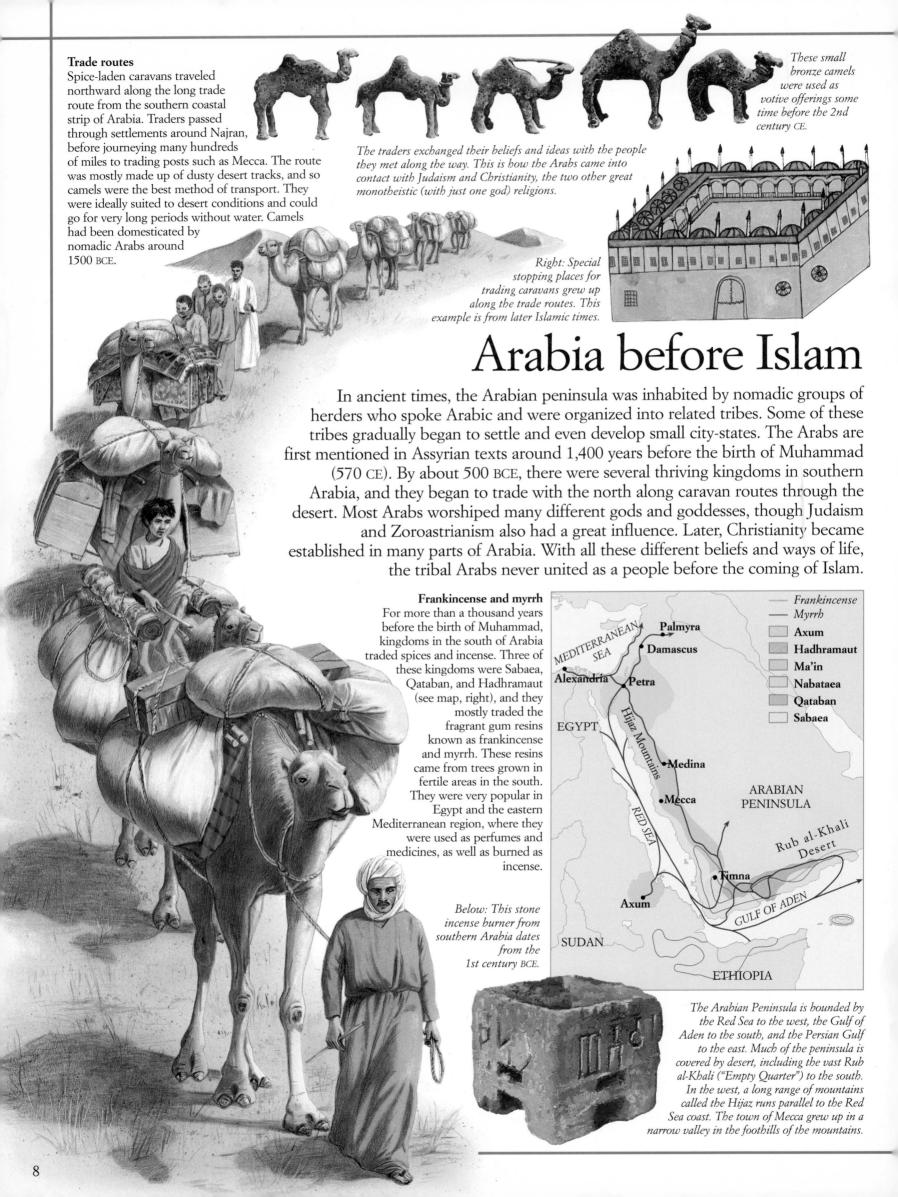

Trade routes

Spice-laden caravans traveled northward along the long trade route from the southern coastal strip of Arabia. Traders passed through settlements around Najran, before journeying many hundreds of miles to trading posts such as Mecca. The route was mostly made up of dusty desert tracks, and so camels were the best method of transport. They were ideally suited to desert conditions and could go for very long periods without water. Camels had been domesticated by nomadic Arabs around 1500 BCE.

These small bronze camels were used as votive offerings some time before the 2nd century CE.

The traders exchanged their beliefs and ideas with the people they met along the way. This is how the Arabs came into contact with Judaism and Christianity, the two other great monotheistic (with just one god) religions.

Right: Special stopping places for trading caravans grew up along the trade routes. This example is from later Islamic times.

Arabia before Islam

In ancient times, the Arabian peninsula was inhabited by nomadic groups of herders who spoke Arabic and were organized into related tribes. Some of these tribes gradually began to settle and even develop small city-states. The Arabs are first mentioned in Assyrian texts around 1,400 years before the birth of Muhammad (570 CE). By about 500 BCE, there were several thriving kingdoms in southern Arabia, and they began to trade with the north along caravan routes through the desert. Most Arabs worshiped many different gods and goddesses, though Judaism and Zoroastrianism also had a great influence. Later, Christianity became established in many parts of Arabia. With all these different beliefs and ways of life, the tribal Arabs never united as a people before the coming of Islam.

Frankincense and myrrh

For more than a thousand years before the birth of Muhammad, kingdoms in the south of Arabia traded spices and incense. Three of these kingdoms were Sabaea, Qataban, and Hadhramaut (see map, right), and they mostly traded the fragrant gum resins known as frankincense and myrrh. These resins came from trees grown in fertile areas in the south. They were very popular in Egypt and the eastern Mediterranean region, where they were used as perfumes and medicines, as well as burned as incense.

Below: This stone incense burner from southern Arabia dates from the 1st century BCE.

Map legend:
- — *Frankincense*
- — *Myrrh*
- Axum
- Hadhramaut
- Ma'in
- Nabataea
- Qataban
- Sabaea

Map labels: MEDITERRANEAN SEA, Palmyra, Damascus, Alexandria, Petra, EGYPT, Hijaz Mountains, Medina, Mecca, RED SEA, ARABIAN PENINSULA, Rub al-Khali Desert, Timna, Axum, GULF OF ADEN, SUDAN, ETHIOPIA

The Arabian Peninsula is bounded by the Red Sea to the west, the Gulf of Aden to the south, and the Persian Gulf to the east. Much of the peninsula is covered by desert, including the vast Rub al-Khali ("Empty Quarter") to the south. In the west, a long range of mountains called the Hijaz runs parallel to the Red Sea coast. The town of Mecca grew up in a narrow valley in the foothills of the mountains.

Nomads and settlers

In pre-Islamic times, the Arabian peninsula was inhabited by two cultural groups. One group was made up of nomadic Bedouins, who moved around the edges of the desert from oasis to oasis. The other was a group of settled communities which grew up around the region's oases. Most of these people spoke Arabic, which belongs to the Semitic group of languages, and they came to be known as Arabs. In the northern regions, they were occasionally invaded by Sumerians, Babylonians, and Persians.

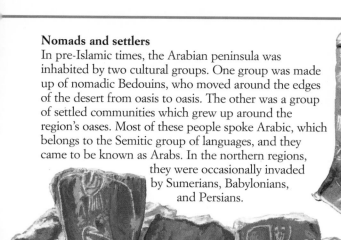

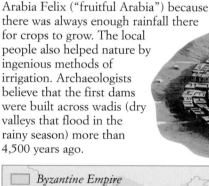

These warriors' graves in the desert of southern Arabia are 4,000 years old.

An inscribed bronze hand from Arabia, dating from the 2nd century CE.

A Persian illustration of a magic tree worshiped by ancient Arabs.

Pre-Islamic gods and goddesses

Before the time of Muhammad, most Arabs worshiped a wide range of gods and goddesses. Among nomadic peoples these deities were tribal, while to many of the settled groups they related to particular regions. Some of the gods were associated with the sun, moon, stars, and planets. Others were demons called jinn, intelligent beings created from smokeless flames. The jinn were usually invisible, but could suddenly appear in human or animal form. In addition, the ancient Arabians held certain rocks, caves, springs, and wells in great respect.

Left: This Arabian funerary statue dates from the 1st century BCE.

The Kaaba stood next to the holy well of Zamzam, whose water was sacred to pilgrims.

Arabia Felix

The ancient Romans called the highland area of the southern peninsula, now part of Yemen, Arabia Felix ("fruitful Arabia") because there was always enough rainfall there for crops to grow. The local people also helped nature by ingenious methods of irrigation. Archaeologists believe that the first dams were built across wadis (dry valleys that flood in the rainy season) more than 4,500 years ago.

Mecca and the Kaaba

The city of Mecca was both a center of commerce and of pilgrimage long before the birth of Muhammad. The Kaaba ("cube") containing "the black stone that fell from heaven in the days of Adam," already stood in the town. Pilgrims traveled vast distances across the desert to offer sacrifices and to worship the holy stone it contained.

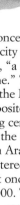

Two great empires ruled the northern fringes of Arabia before the time of Muhammad. Each empire had its greatest ruler during the 6th century BCE: Emperor Justinian ruled the Byzantines, and King Khosrow reigned over the Sassanids.

Byzantine Empire
Sassanian Empire

BLACK SEA
CASPIAN SEA
•Constantinople
CENTRAL ASIA
ANATOLIA
MEDITERRANEAN SEA
Ctesiphon
NORTH AFRICA
•Jerusalem
PERSIA
Alexandria•
ARABIA
•**Persepolis**
•**Medina**
•**Mecca**
YEMEN
INDIAN OCEAN
ETHIOPIA

The rose-red city

A poet once famously called the ancient city of Petra, in modern Jordan, "a rose-red city, half as old as time." This was the capital city of the Nabataeans (see the map opposite). Petra was a great trading center, at the northern end of the caravan routes from southern Arabia, and could only be entered through a narrow gorge. It once had a population of 30,000. Today its ruins are a great tourist attraction.

A massive rock-cut tomb in Petra, probably the burial place of a Nabataean king.

Sassanids

In the northeast of the Arabian peninsula, the Sassanid dynasty ruled an empire based on ancient Persia (modern Iran) from 224 CE. The Sassanids were Zoroastrians, following the teachings of a Persian prophet of the 6th century BCE. They were named after Sasan, the grandfather of their first ruler, Ardashir. He ruled from his capital of Ctesiphon, on the River Tigris in modern Iraq. The Sassanids were frequently at war with the Romans and Byzantines, but they were finally defeated by Arabs just fifteen years after the beginning of the Islamic era.

This rock relief shows the first Sassanid ruler Ardashir (ruled 224-241) being given his power by the supreme Zoroastrian god, Ahura Mazda. The spirit of evil, Ahriman, is being crushed beneath their horses' hooves.

Byzantine Empire

The Byzantine Empire (Eastern Roman Empire) had its capital in Constantinople. It came into existence when Emperor Constantine decided in 330 CE to move his capital from Rome to Byzantium (modern Istanbul), which was renamed Constantinople after him. After the last Western Roman emperor was deposed in 476, the Byzantine Empire survived and continued for almost a thousand years. It was the center of Orthodox Christianity.

Hagia Sophia, the Church of Holy Wisdom, in Constantinople, was built by Justinian I and dedicated in 537. It took 10,000 masons, carpenters, sculptors, and artists over five years to complete.

The Prophet

Muslims believe that Muhammad (c.570–632 CE) was the last and seal of the prophets of Allah. He was born in the town of Mecca, now in Saudi Arabia, and led an ordinary life as a boy and young man. At the age of forty, however, he received his first revelation from Allah. He then spent the rest of his life teaching people about the truths that were revealed to him. In 622, Muhammad traveled to Medina, and this journey marks the first year of the Islamic calendar and the beginning of the Muslim era. The Prophet urged his people to give up their pagan idols and turn to the one true God, Allah. His message included the need for a good, fair society based on brotherhood rather than tribal differences and without the extremes of great wealth and poverty.

Above: Muhammad with the prophet Moses. Muslims believe that Allah revealed his messages to twenty-five prophets, but that Muhammad received the complete and final revelation.

The baby Muhammad, shown in a 16th-century Ottoman miniature.

Below: Aishah with Muhammad's daughter Fatima and another of his wives, Umma Salama. Their faces are veiled.

The Prophet's family
Muhammad's parents belonged to the Hashim clan, which was part of the Quraysh tribe. This was the leading tribe in the trading city of Mecca, and the Hashim clan were said to trace their ancestors back to Ibrahim and his son Ismail. Muhammad's father, a merchant named Abdullah, died before the prophet was born. His mother, Amina, also died when he was just six years old.

The Bedouin probably lived in tents similar to those they use today.

Merchants in southern Arabia.

Youth
After his mother died, Muhammad was looked after by his grandfather, Abd-al-Muttalib. When he also died, eight-year-old Muhammad went to live with his uncle, Abu Talib, who was then head of the Hashim clan. At first the young Muhammad learned to herd sheep and camels, and later he worked for his uncle as a merchant. They traveled together on caravan journeys across Arabia to Syria. Because of his honesty and fair dealings, Muhammad became known as al-Amin, "the trusted one."

Childhood influences
Following Quraysh custom, the baby Muhammad was given to a Bedouin foster mother and wet nurse, named Halimah. The Quraysh, who had lived a nomadic life in the desert before settling in towns, believed that this was the way to make children healthy and strong. The pure desert air was thought to be good for them. Around 576, Muhammad's real mother took him to see his grandparents in Medina, but on the way she fell ill and died.

An early manuscript of the Qur'an written in ancient Kufic script.

The first calling
While he was married to Khadijah, Muhammad began to devote more and more time to quiet meditation. He would go to Mount Hira, which overlooked Mecca, and it was there in 610 that he received his first revelation. Muhammad was praying in a cave when he heard a voice calling his name. The angel Jibril (Gabriel, below right) appeared and told Muhammad that he was to be the messenger of God. Then the angel showed Muhammad some words and told him to recite them. He replied that he was not a learned man and could not read the words, but Jibril insisted and Muhammad suddenly felt that he knew the words and could recite them.

Marriage
Muhammad went to work for a wealthy widow, Khadijah, helping her with her trading interests. At the age of twenty-five, he married Khadijah, and they had four daughters and two sons, both of whom died at a young age. Muhammad took no other wives while Khadijah was alive. Later, he married Aishah, the young daughter of his closest friend, Abu Bakr. She was a kind and generous woman, and became the Prophet's favorite wife.

The Revelations
After his first vision, Muhammad went on receiving revelations for the rest of his life. He did not always see the angel Jibril, and sometimes he just heard a voice speaking to him. Some revelations occurred when he was praying, but others came to him while he was going about his daily life. After each revelation, he would repeat the words to his friends. They wrote some down on parchment, pieces of wood, or palm leaves, but most they simply memorized. The revelations were later collected together to form the Qur'an.

Following Muhammad

The first people to hear about the revelations were Muhammad's first wife Khadijah, his young cousin Ali, and his servant Zayd. When the Prophet started taking his message to others in Mecca, he gained followers among laborers, poor people, and slaves. Many wealthier people disliked and distrusted him, thinking that he would ruin their comfortable lives. They soon began to plot against him.

Muhammad's early followers invited him to dine with them so that they could listen to his teachings.

The Night Journey

One night Muhammad was woken from sleep by the angel Jibril. The angel told him to mount a winged animal similar to a horse, which took him to the Temple of Abu Bakr, in Jerusalem. There he was taken up to the seven heavens and met other prophets from the past, including Musa and Isa. Then Muhammad went on alone and approached the throne of Allah, before returning to Mecca on his winged beast. When they heard of this, the Prophet's followers were not sure whether the journey had physically taken place or was a spiritual experience.

In this Persian miniature of the Night Journey, Muhammad's mount is shown with a human head.

The Hijra

Though he was gaining more followers, opposition to Muhammad among the Quraysh of Mecca continued to grow. But his words had spread beyond his home town. In 622, some of the elders of the town of Yathrib invited him to move there and teach their people. Muhammad agreed to go, and his journey became known as the Hijra, or "migration." After he arrived in Yathrib, the town took a new name – Madinat al-Nabi ("city of the prophet"), or Medina.

Above: The faithful building Muhammad's mosque. Additions were made later to house his subsequent wives.

The beginning of Islam

Within a very short time of being in Medina, Muhammad succeeded in creating a unity between the native Medinese Arabs and the Meccans who had joined him there. In the years that followed, he became established as a prophet and enjoyed unrestricted power over the town. He set about building a house that was to be his home and a place of worship, the first mosque. Public services were held there every Friday, and times were allotted for private prayer on a daily basis. He also established the taking up of alms for the poor.

Above: Muhammad's mosque and tomb in Medina, from a 16th-century Moroccan text.

Muhammad and his followers returned to Mecca in 630.

Destruction of the idols

After eight years and many attempts to make peace with his opponents in Mecca, Muhammad finally returned in triumph. He took a large army of 10,000 followers with him, and the Meccans had no choice but to accept him. Having claimed the city, Muhammad pardoned his Quraysh opponents. Then the Prophet went to the Kaaba, entered the shrine, and destroyed all its idols.

Right: Muhammad and his cousin Ali remove the idols from the Kaaba, including the stone statuette of the pagan god Hubal.

Muhammad's death

Muhammad made a final pilgrimage to Mecca in 632 and then returned to Medina. On June 8th, his father-in-law Abu Bakr invited him to lead prayers in the mosque. But Muhammad was feeling unwell. He went into the house and lay down in Aisha's arms, where he died. He was buried at that very spot, which is now part of the Medina mosque and a place of pilgrimage.

Right: close companions of Muhammad weep at his death.

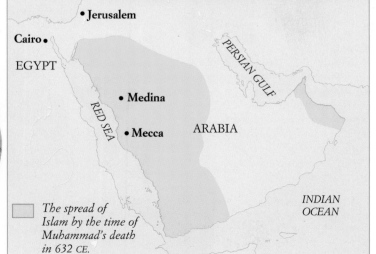

• Jerusalem

Cairo •

EGYPT

PERSIAN GULF

RED SEA

• Medina

• Mecca

ARABIA

INDIAN OCEAN

The spread of Islam by the time of Muhammad's death in 632 CE.

The Qur'an

The Qur'an is made up of 114 *suras* (chapters), each containing a number of *ayas* (verses). The chapters are arranged according to length, with the longest at the beginning. According to tradition, the first caliph, or ruler, ordered Muhammad's secretary to collect and arrange the writings after the Prophet's death. Today, all copies of the book are treated with great respect and are often put on a special bookrest for reading. Since the Qur'an was written in Arabic, no translation has been given any weight and may not be recited during prayer.

Yemenite man studying the Qur'an.

Right: This Hadith was written by a Turkish master of calligraphy.

The Hadiths

The Hadiths are "traditions" recording the sayings and teachings of the Prophet, as well as stories about him. These were collected and checked by Islamic scholars two hundred years after Muhammad's death. There are six major collections, the most famous being that of al-Bukhari (810–70), who traveled widely in search of examples.

Allah

This word is formed from the Arabic *al-Ilah*, which means "the God." All Muslims believe that Allah is the one, eternal, all-powerful God. He created the whole of the universe and everything in it, and there is no other like him. There are ninety-nine Beautiful Names of God, such as *al-Rahman* (the Merciful), and these are recited during worship.

A decorative tile with the inscription "Allah."

Basic teachings

Muslims are guided by Allah's message. This was revealed first to the Prophet Muhammad and then to all believers through the Qur'an. This holy book is the basis for all the teachings of Islam, including its religious, legal, and social rules. Muslims also follow the life and example of Muhammad through the traditions handed down by the Prophet and collections of his sayings. Islamic teachings and beliefs include a set of five special duties which all Muslims must perform. Islam is a complete way of life, and its teachings cover all aspects of belief and behavior.

The Arabic shahada *is written on this tile. It reads: "There is no god but Allah, and Muhammad is the messenger of Allah."*

The Five Pillars of Islam

Each of the five pillars is a basic duty, and together the duties form a support for the whole structure of Islam. The first duty is a declaration of faith, called *shahada*. Muslims say the special words (see above) first thing in the morning and last thing at night. They are also said at the birth of a new baby.

Salah

Ritual prayers, or *salah*, form the second of the five pillars. The prayers are said kneeling in the direction of Mecca (see left). They are performed five times a day: just before sunrise, just after midday, during the afternoon when shadows have lengthened, just after sunset, and during the hours of darkness. The prayer times avoid the exact times of sunrise, midday, and sunset, because these were once associated with sun worship. Muslims wash themselves in preparation for the prayers.

Below: This illustration was painted on an Egyptian villager's wall to celebrate a pilgrimage to Mecca.

Giving to others

The third of the five pillars is called *zakah*, which literally means "cleansing." This is the duty of giving to those who are less fortunate than oneself. The basic amount of *zakah* is considered to be one fortieth of a person's wealth, though it is good to give more if possible. Rich Muslims "cleanse" or purify their wealth by giving generously but without making a show of it.

These men are saying a prayer of thanks before breaking their fast at the end of Ramadan.

Fasting

The fourth pillar involves fasting during Ramadan, the ninth month of the Islamic calendar. For thirty days healthy adult Muslims do not eat or drink anything during the hours of daylight between dawn and dusk. Children, pregnant and nursing mothers, menstruating women, and sick people do not have to fast. During the fast, almost all Muslims get up before dawn to eat a special breakfast.

Pilgrimage

The fifth duty is to go on a special pilgrimage to Mecca, called hajj (see pages 56–57). All Muslims must try to make this journey at least once in their lifetime, unless this would cause hardship to their dependants.

The Day of Judgment

Muslims believe that when people die, they face a Day of Judgment. Those believers who led a good life are rewarded for ever in paradise, which is described in the Qur'an as a beautiful garden full of flowers and flowing water. Unbelievers who fail the test must go to eternal hell, which is described as a place of torment beneath the Earth's crust.

The angel Israfil sounds his trumpet on the Day of Judgment.

Right: Figure of a jinn, or genie. Pre-Islamic Arabs also believed in these strange beings.

Left: Sinners suffer the fires of hell in this 15th-century miniature.

Jihad

The word *jihad* comes from the Arabic for "effort" or "striving." In the personal, spiritual sense, jihad means striving to serve Allah and striving against sin. The term is also used to mean a "holy war" undertaken by Muslims against unbelievers. This does not mean forcing others to accept Islam or become Muslims, but striving to bring about a just society where Muslims can live as they wish and everyone can live in peace.

Below: A father shaves his baby's head. Traditionally, the equivalent of the weight of hair in gold or silver is given to the poor.

Muhammad's army. The Prophet himself fought many battles.

Angels

Angels are the servants and messengers of Allah, made from light. Jibril is the most important, since he revealed Allah's words to Muhammad. Mikail watches over holy places. Izra'il takes away people's souls when they die. Ridwan is the guardian of paradise, while Malik watches over hell. There are also demons made of flames, called jinns, who can take on various forms and be good or bad. The Devil, called Iblis or Shaytan (Satan), is the enemy of all humans and constantly tries to make them do evil.

Shari'a

Shari'a is the Islamic law, or "path," which is based on the Qur'an, the Hadiths, and the work of scholars in the first two centuries of Islam. Rules of behavior are often divided into five categories: those which must be obeyed, such as keeping the five pillars; those which are recommended, such as saying extra prayers; those which must be decided by a person's own conscience; those which are disapproved of, such as divorce; and those which are strictly forbidden, such as worshipping false gods.

Birth

Every child is seen as a gift from Allah. Shortly after birth, the father whispers the words of the call to prayer into his child's right ear and the command to worship in the left ear. One of the oldest relatives rubs a little honey or sweet juice on the baby's gums, making the child "sweet" and kind. Babies are named when they are seven days old, and baby boys are circumcised.

Food and drink

For Muslims, some foods are halal (allowed) and others are haram (forbidden). Forbidden foods include pork, meat with blood in it, the meat of an animal that has died due to disease or old age, the meat of flesh-eating animals, or the meat of any animal that has not been killed by the halal method. By this method, Muslim butchers cut the jugular vein in an animal's neck with a sharp knife while calling the name of Allah. All forms of alcohol are forbidden. Stamps on food (see left) guarantee that the food is allowed.

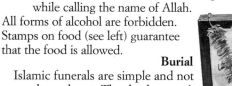

An Ottoman miniature of a Muslim scholar.

Dress

Muslims believe that clothing should always be clean and modest. Men should never look flashy and should not wear silk or gold jewelry. When praying, they must be covered at least from the waist to the knees. Women's clothing should not be too revealing or attention-seeking.

Mannequins model Muslim outfits in a Cairo shop window.

Burial

Islamic funerals are simple and not costly or showy. The dead person's body is wrapped in a shroud of white sheets and usually carried to the cemetery. Coffins are only used if they are necessary for health reasons. The body is put in the grave on its right side, with the face toward Mecca. The grave is usually marked with a simple headstone.

A Muslim grave in Srinagar, India.

The first caliph

Since Muhammad left no male heirs and no indication as to who should succeed him, it was left to his closest friends and supporters to choose someone. They chose Abu Bakr and named him caliph (from the Arabic for "successor" or "deputy"). Though followers of Islam in Medina and Mecca were happy with this, others refused to recognize the caliph's authority or pay the poor tax that Muhammad had instituted. Abu Bakr acted quickly against these rebels, sending armed bands to Yemen and other places of unrest. By the time he died, the entire Arabian peninsula was under Muslim control.

Abu Bakr (c.573–634) was the Prophet's father-in-law and closest friend.

This later Persian miniature shows a Muslim giving alms to a poor man. The early rebels objected to this form of tax.

Conquests

The second and third caliphs, Umar I and Uthman, continued the work of Abu Bakr. Damascus surrendered in 635, raids were made into Persia, Palestine and present-day Iraq were conquered by 640, and Egypt was taken from the Byzantines in 645. Uthman, who belonged to the powerful Umayya family, was an early convert and married two of Muhammad's daughters. He led the Islamic community for twelve years before he was murdered by rebellious troops in 656.

Early Muslim soldiers rode horses or camels and were lightly armed. Most military attacks were small-scale raids.

Arab expansion and the Umayyads

After Muhammad's death in 632, successors were chosen to lead the growing group of Muslims. They were called caliphs. The first four caliphs followed Muhammad's example closely, and during their time, the world of Islam expanded quickly. The fourth caliph, Ali, belonged to the same clan of the Quraysh tribe as Muhammad. He was opposed by many Muslims, including those of the Umayyad family, who came from a different clan. The Umayyad dynasty came to power in 661 and ruled from Damascus for almost ninety years. During this time Islam continued to expand.

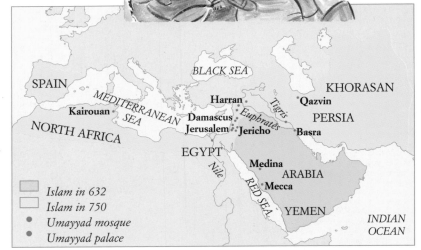

Islam in 632
Islam in 750
● Umayyad mosque
● Umayyad palace

The spread of Islam during the 7th and early 8th centuries.

Civil war

After Uthman's murder, the people of Medina recognized Ali ibn Abi Talib (c.598–661) as the fourth caliph. Ali was Muhammad's cousin and had become his son-in-law by marrying the Prophet's daughter Fatima. Others, however, joined members of the Umayya family in opposing Ali. Disagreements led to a five-year civil war, which was brought to an end when Ali was assassinated by a member of the Kharijite sect. The majority of Muslims then agreed to recognize Muawiyah (c.602–680), an Umayyad, as caliph.

Left: In this Persian miniature, the angel Jibril announces to Ali that he will be the Prophet's successor.

Below: Work on the Great Mosque in the Umayyad capital of Damascus began in 706. It was built on the site of the former Basilica of John the Baptist.

Mosaic from a courtyard wall at the Great Mosque of Damascus.

Early Umayyads

Muawiyah had been governor of Syria for twenty years when he became caliph in 661, and he decided to make Damascus the new capital of Islam. He was an experienced administrator, and he divided the Islamic empire into provinces, with his kinsmen as governors. The Syrian army controlled the conquered territories, and Arab tribal rivalries were kept in check. Muawiyah chose his son Yazid to be his successor, which proved to be very unpopular since earlier caliphs had been elected by elders.

Ornamental jug from Umayyad Damascus.

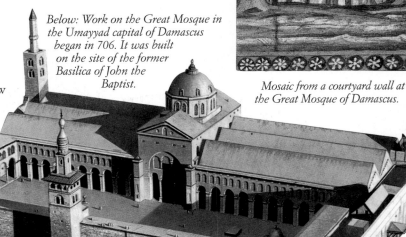

Husayn's martyrdom

There was civil war for twelve years after Muawiyah's death. The Umayyads were faced with widespread opposition, especially from the Shi'ites. They believed that Ali's younger son Husayn, grandson of Muhammad, should be Islamic leader. After Husayn and members of his family were massacred by Yazid's forces in 680, the Shi'ites began to act more and more as an entirely separate group within the Islamic community. The massacre is remembered by Shi'ites to this day at the festival of Ashura (see page 46).

Below: Painting of the massacre of Husayn.

This 8th-century bathhouse, inspired by Roman examples, was part of an Umayyad desert palace in Jordan.

Desert palaces

The Umayyad caliphs had a city palace near the Great Mosque in Damascus, and there were palaces in other major cities. In addition, smaller Umayyad palaces have been found in desert regions of Syria, Jordan, and Palestine. These may have served as country retreats for ruling Arab families, helping to keep them in touch with Bedouin nomads. The palaces may also have served as hunting lodges and forts.

Right: Ornamental window in an Umayyad palace at Jericho, in Palestine.

Shi'ite standard bearing the names of Allah, Muhammad, and Ali.

Right: This remarkable mosaic was found in an Umayyad palace. Beneath the tree, the two browsing gazelles represent the Islamic world at peace, while the attacking lion symbolizes war.

Right: Statue of a woman from the palace at Jericho, made around 740.

Abd al-Malik

Abd al-Malik (646–705) became fifth Umayyad caliph in 685. During his rule, the Umayyad caliphate reached its peak. Muslim armies gained territory as far away from Damascus as Spain to the west and central Asia and northern India to the east. Arabic became the official state language, and Arabic coins were introduced. A regular postal service connected Damascus with the provincial capitals, where Arabs had replaced local officials. At the same time, many non-Arabs also converted to Islam.

Right: This statue shows a caliph dressed as an ancient Sasanian king. Historians think it may be al-Walid II, who was murdered in 744.

Coin showing Abd al-Malik holding the sword of Islam.

Decline of the Umayyads

After the Syrian army was defeated by the Byzantines in 717, the Umayyads went into decline. The Berbers rebelled against Arab rule in North Africa during the 740s, and the Umayyads were also weakened by disputes between Arab tribes. There were constant quarrels over who should become caliph, and rebellions within the Umayyad family made things worse.

Defeat and murder

In 750, Caliph Marwan II was defeated by the Abbasid general Abu Muslim at the Battle of the Great Zab River, a tributary of the Tigris. Eighty Umayyad princes were then murdered at a banquet in Jaffa, along with their wives and children. Just one survived, and he escaped to North Africa and established himself as ruler in Spain (see page 20). But in Asia, Umayyad rule was at an end.

Above: Inside the Dome of the Rock. This was built in Jerusalem by Abd al-Malik in 691 on the site where Muhammad ascended to heaven on his Night Journey (see page 11).

15

The Abbasids

Taking over from the Umayyads, the Abbasids ruled the Islamic world from 750 to 1258. They moved the capital of the empire to Baghdad, which quickly became a magnificent city and center of power. During the first hundred years of their reign, their prestige grew as great advances were made in science, commerce, and the arts. This period is remembered throughout the Muslim world, and by Iraqis especially, as a golden age and pinnacle of the Islamic past. For centuries the Abbasid caliphs ruled over a unified empire that stretched from the Atlantic Ocean to central Asia. Their power and unity were lost during the 10th century, however, and they were never recovered.

This gilt silver dish, dating from the 9th or 10th century, has designs based on the simurgh, a mythical bird of ancient Persia.

Harun al-Rashid takes a bath, in a scene from The Thousand and One Nights.

The early years

The Abbasids took their name from al-Abbas, a Hashimite uncle of the Prophet Muhammad who died around 653. Al-Abbas had fought Muhammad at the Battle of Badr in 624, but later joined his nephew's cause and helped him on his return to Mecca. By 718, a great-grandson of al-Abbas was trying to gain control of the expanding Islamic Empire, and as a member of the clan of Hashim and a descendant of Muhammad, he gained support from the Shi'ites and others. Thirty years later, there was open revolt, and in 750, after the overthrow of the Umayyads, Abu Abbas al-Saffah became the first Abbasid caliph in Kufa.

Plan of Abbasid Baghdad

TIGRIS · Syria Gate · Khurasan Gate · Guard House · Palace · Mosque · Kufa Gate · Basra Gate

Round city

The second Abbasid caliph, al-Mansur (c.709–75), was the son of a great-grandson of Muhammad. Al-Mansur decided that his dynasty needed a new capital for its empire, and so in 762 he started work at the site of an ancient village. The caliph named the capital Madinat al-Salam, meaning "City of Peace," but people went on using the old name of Baghdad. The round city had two sets of mud-brick walls surrounding a ring of residences and government offices, with the caliph's palace and a mosque in the center. Settlements grew up outside the walls of the city, which, by 800 CE, may have had as many as half a million inhabitants.

The Thousand and One Nights

Legend surrounds the fifth Abbasid caliph, Harun al-Rashid (ruled 786–809), because of the fabulous descriptions of him and his Baghdad court in *The Thousand and One Nights*. Though the descriptions were exaggerated, they were based on truth. Harun's wife Zubaydah, who also belonged to the Abbasid family, would only allow food to be served in dishes of gold and silver studded with gems. Harun loved music and poetry and became a generous patron of the arts.

Above: This 13th-century miniature shows scholars and teachers with their students in Baghdad.

Wall painting from an Abbasid caliph's palace showing dancers pouring wine.

Astronomy advanced greatly under al-Mamun. This scene shows an astronomer holding an astrolabe.

Art

The Abbasid period was influential in the development of Islamic art. Textiles were important and were designed both for clothing and furnishings. Harun-al-Rashid is said to have had a wardrobe of 10,000 caftans, 8,000 coats, and 4,000 turbans! Abbasid potters made fine, brightly colored tableware, while metalworkers devised ways of improving their wares with wonderful patterns.

Science and philosophy

After the death of Harun al-Rashid, two of his sons fought over the caliphate. The dispute was won by al-Mamun (ruled 813–33), and during his reign Islamic culture experienced a golden age. Science and philosophy were of particular importance, and al-Mamun established the famous House of Science in Baghdad, which included a scientific library and became a center of learning. Philosophy and literature also flourished.

An illustration of one of the earliest literary forms in Arabic – the animal fable. In it, a jackal named Dimna is talking to a lion.

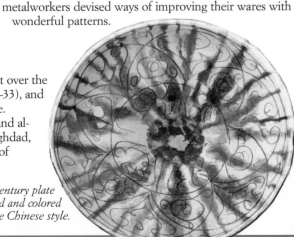

This 9th-century plate was engraved and colored in the Chinese style.

Trade

The Abbasid Empire stretched across North Africa, through the Middle East to central Asia. Trade with the Far East was helped by the great Silk Road, which stretched all the way from Baghdad to Chang'an in China. Trade flourished throughout the various provinces of the empire, providing wealth for the caliphs. This led to a banking system that allowed a letter of credit issued in Baghdad to be honored in Kairouan (in modern Tunisia) or Samarkand (in Uzbekistan). Increase in trade generated work for craftworkers of all kinds.

Left: Merchants at work.

Left: 9th-century glass bottle from the Middle East. This style of colored decoration was popular in Samarra.

Right: A local governor listens to a complaint.

Map

ATLANTIC OCEAN

BLACK SEA

• Rome
• Constantinople

• Samarcanda
• Cordoba
• Tabriz Nishapur • Merw
Tunis •
• Balkh
• Fez Kairouan MEDITERRANEAN SEA Damascus • Samarra • • Herat
Mulai Idris • Baghdad
NORTH AFRICA • Jerusalem
Cairo • PERSIA
EGYPT

RED SEA

• Mecca ARABIAN
ARABIA SEA

☐ Byzantine Empire
☐ Abbasid Empire's greatest extent
☐ Abbasid Empire's nucleus after 850

Samarra

In 836, al-Mutasim moved the Abbasid capital upstream along the River Tigris to Samarra. It was as if he wanted a new start for the caliphate. At Samarra he built a vast palace, with a complex of interconnected courts and gardens. There were several lesser palaces for army commanders, a ceremonial avenue, and a colossal Great Mosque, which for many centuries was the largest in the world. Samarra remained the capital until 892, when the caliphate returned to Baghdad.

Right: Beautiful wall tile from the caliph's palace at Samarra.

Spiral minaret of the Great Mosque at Samarra, completed in 852.

African slaves in Arabia.

Above: A 10th-century glazed earthenware bowl shows a cavalryman wielding a sword.

Governing the empire

During the 9th century, the caliphs spent more time in their lavish palaces and so became removed from the people they ruled. Another son of Harun al-Rashid, al-Mutasim (ruled 833–42), appointed governors in the provinces and brought non-Muslim Berber, Slav, and Turkish troops into his army. The soldiers converted to Islam, and their officers quickly learned how to gain control over their ultimate commander, the caliph. Clashes broke out in Baghdad between Turkish mercenaries and Arab soldiers.

Persian illustration showing the Mongol siege of Baghdad. A Mongol commander is crossing the Tigris River on a bridge made of chained boats.

Decline and fall

Several disastrous events weakened Abbasid power. In the late 9th century, there was a major slave revolt in what is now Iraq. Military power was lost when Shi'ite Buyids from northern Persia marched into Baghdad in 945. From then on, much of the empire was ruled by local dynasties. In 1055, the Seljuks overpowered the Buyids and took control, leaving the caliph to act as a religious figurehead. Finally, in 1258, Baghdad fell to invading Mongols commanded by the non-Muslim Hülagü, a grandson of Ghengis Khan. The last Abbasid caliph, al-Musta'sim, was executed.

Sufism

Sufis are Muslims mystics who search for a close, personal relationship and oneness with Allah. In order to achieve this, Sufis believe in leading a simple life of self-denial, and in the past many gave up all their worldly goods, took a vow of poverty, and begged in order to live. Many Sufis repeat words of the Qur'an, in their attempt to reach a higher level of consciousness, or ecstasy. Through the centuries, they have had many opponents within the Muslim world, but they helped to spread Islam and still have an important influence. In addition, many of the greatest Muslim poets have been Sufis.

Ceramic decoration from the tomb of Abdallah al-Ansari, a Sufi author and saint who died in 1089 CE. His shrine in Herat, Afghanistan, is an important pilgrimage site.

Dressed in wool

In Arabic, Islamic mysticism is called *tasawwuf*, which originally meant "to dress in wool." In the same way, the terms *Sufi* and *Sufism* come from Arabic *suf*, meaning "wool." The use of the words came about because the early Muslim mystics often wore simple woolen robes.

A 19th-century illustration of an Indonesian Sufi wearing a woolen robe.

Origins

Sufism began as an organized movement in the 8th century. It developed among Muslims who were unhappy about the attitudes of those around them. They felt that many Muslims were thinking too much about the everyday comforts and problems and not enough about Islam and Allah. The early Sufis wanted to experience Allah in their own lives and decided that they needed to take their own mystic path by meditating and denying themselves worldly pleasures.

Above: This ceramic plate, made and painted in 1210 in Iran, shows a young man in a mystical state. He is watched by others as he contemplates his own soul.

Right: A Muslim prince visits a Sufi hermit's cave to ask for the mystic's advice and blessing.

A new path

The Sufis increasingly wanted to find a new path to Islam. This led some other Muslims to think that the Sufis were going against the regulations laid down by the Shari'a (or traditional Islamic law, see page 13). This was not really the case, though the Sufis' beliefs were in conflict with those of many Islamic rulers. Sufis believed that a ruler should be the person most qualified in spiritual terms and that he should lead a simple life.

Sufis used prayer beads to count their repetitions as early as the 8th century.

An 18th-century illustration of Khwaja Khidr.

Pre-Islamic cults

The Sufis knew many tales from pre-Islamic times, and they kept them alive by reciting them. This meant that earlier cults became included in Islamic traditions. One of these was the cult of Khwaja Khidr, who had first appeared in the Mesopotamian *Epic of Gilgamesh* before 2000 BCE. He was associated with springtime and was thought to help people lost at sea as well as in the desert.

Masters and followers

By the 12th century, the Sufis had formed many groups, each under the leadership of a *shaikh*, or "master," who was the most gifted among them. These Sufic communities then organized themselves into orders, whose members were known as *faqirs* (meaning "poor ones," because they had no worldly wealth). A Spanish-born master named Ibn al-Arabi (1165–1240), later known as "the greatest shaikh," taught the Sufic theory that all beings exist in one unity.

Ways of worship

Meditation and mental struggle have always been an important part of the Sufic approach to Islam. Many Sufis were very strict, allowing themselves little sleep, or food. Along with ritual prayers, fasting became part of their spiritual lives. Many prayers were based on repeating the beautiful names of Allah, or forms of words such as "Allah is most great," over and over again. This *dhikr*, or "remembrance," is often accompanied by special breathing or movements.

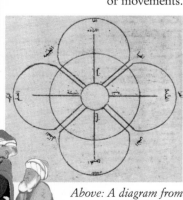

Above: A diagram from one of Ibn al-Arabi's works showing many aspects coming out of one central unity.

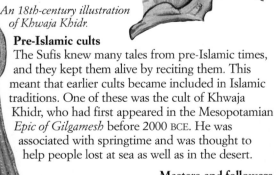

This 17th-century Mogul painting shows a group of Sufic masters.

Left: Sufi musicians, from a 16th-century Persian illustration.

In The Conference of the Birds, *an allegorical poem by Farid ad-Din Attar, a flock of birds goes on a dangerous journey to see their king Simurgh (right). Thirty survive and discover that they are Simurgh themselves (si murgh means thirty birds).*

Dervishes

Unlike other Muslims, Sufis use music and dance as a way of reaching a higher level of consciousness. An order known as the Mevleviyya, or Dervishes (from the Persian *darvis* meaning "poor"), whirl themselves into a trance to the steady rhythm of tambourines and pipes. In this way, the Whirling Dervishes (see right) attempt to become one with Allah as they lose consciousness of who they are. Their movements may also represent Earth and the other planets orbiting the Sun.

Poetry

There have been many great Sufic poets, and their work has influenced the whole of Islam. One of the greatest was Jalal al-Din Rumi (1207–73), a Persian who went to live in Konya, in present-day Turkey. His mausoleum, the Green Dome, is still a place of pilgrimage today. Rumi wrote a large collection of lyric poetry, including one vast poem that extends over six volumes. He is also known as the founder of the Mevleviyya.

This 16th-century painting shows a cow miraculously bowing at the sight of the poet Rumi.

Missionaries

From the 13th century on, Sufi missionaries helped to spread Islam in Asia and Africa. Members of several orders settled in India, while others helped to convert pagan Turks to Islam. The Naqshbandiyya order was very influential in central and east Asia, including China. In Africa, the Tijaniyya order, named after its Algerian founder, helped extend Islam to Nigeria and Senegal.

Left: Page from a Mamluk copy of al-Ghazali's treatise Revival of the Religious Sciences, *one of classical Islam's most celebrated books.*

A modern-day shaikh of the Naqshbandiyya order raising his hands in prayer.

Right: Dervishes in Omdurman, Sudan, where an Islamic University was founded in 1961.

Following the Qur'an

The Sufis' music, chanting, and dancing were disliked by orthodox religious teachers. Nevertheless, most Sufis tried very hard not to go against orthodox teaching and to keep to the Shari'a. Like all Muslims, they took their beliefs from the divine revelations of the Qur'an. They studied the sacred book very closely, finding many new meanings in every verse. The influential Sufic scholar Abu Hamid al-Ghazali (1058–1111) taught that all Muslims must follow traditional law as well as the Qur'an.

Sufism today

Many Sufi orders still exist throughout the Islamic world, though some may not have as many members as in the past. There are several main international orders, including the Qadiriyya (named after a 12th-century Baghdad teacher) and the Naqshbandiyya. In India and Africa there are important local orders. It is thought that many Sunni Muslim rulers are members of a Sufi order.

Islamic Spain

Muslim rule of the Iberian peninsula began in the 8th century and reached its peak two hundred years later, when al-Andalus (Andalusia) was under the rule of the caliphs of Cordoba. At that time, the beliefs and customs of non-Muslims were tolerated, but the situation changed later when Muslim leaders began fighting each other and the Christian reconquest of Spain gathered pace. By the 13th century, Muslim-controlled territory was reduced to the Nasrid kingdom of Granada. The last Muslim ruler in Andalusia, Muhammad XII, handed Granada over to the Christian kings in 1492.

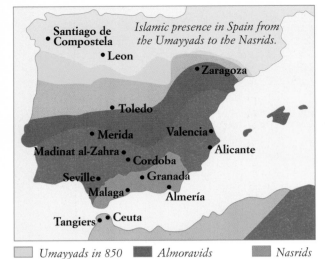

Islamic presence in Spain from the Umayyads to the Nasrids.

- Santiago de Compostela
- Leon
- Zaragoza
- Toledo
- Merida
- Valencia
- Madinat al-Zahra
- Alicante
- Cordoba
- Seville
- Granada
- Malaga
- Almería
- Tangiers
- Ceuta

Umayyads in 850	Almoravids
Umayyads in 950	Almohads
	Nasrids

Muslims in Spain

In 711, a Berber general led a Muslim force of Arabs and North Africans across the strait to Gibraltar. The Muslims moved north and soon captured most of the Iberian peninsula, establishing the province of al-Andalus. In 756, an Umayyad prince named Abd al-Rahman escaped the Abbasid massacre of his family in Damascus (see page 15) and took control of al-Andalus as emir (or "commander"), making Cordoba his capital.

Left: Poets and scholars in the garden of a Jewish physician who acted as a counsellor to the caliph of Cordoba.

The caliphs and science

Interest in science grew in the royal courts of the 10th century. It was during the reign of the first caliph Abd al-Rahman III that a new Arabic translation of the great botanical work of Dioscorides was begun (see page 34). The translation from Greek was the joint work of Muslim, Christian, and Jewish scholars. The caliph's son, who succeeded him as al-Hakam II, showed an even stronger interest in astronomy, medicine, and mathematics, sending emissaries to Egypt and present-day Iraq to collect works for his great library.

This bronze animal was made for a Cordoba fountain in the late 10th century.

Cordoban culture

Al-Andalus reached the height of its power during the reign of Abd al-Rahman III (891–961), who became emir in 912 and declared himself caliph in 929. It was under his rule that Cordoba became a noted center of learning and the arts, including astronomy, medicine, and literature. The capital city had paved, well-lit streets and was known for its public baths and libraries.

Left: Ivory casket made in Cordoba around 1100.

Non-Muslims

During the Umayyad period in Iberia (756–1031), Muslims, Christians, and Jews lived closely together. Ordinary non-Muslims were treated as second-class citizens, which led inevitably to tensions. Nevertheless, educated non-Muslims were able to contribute to the caliphate's success in Cordoba, especially in the arts. Christians also took part in government, and Jews were valued for their scholarship.

The interior of a Jewish synagogue in northern Spain, from a 14th-century manuscript.

Left: Abu Qasim (known in the West as Abulcasis) was physician to al-Hakam II. His medical treatise Al Tasrif *was for centuries an important surgical textbook.*

Below: Architectural detail above a 10th-century portal in the Great Mosque at Cordoba.

Architecture

The two great monuments of the Cordoba caliphate were the Great Mosque and the palace complex of Madinat al-Zahra. The Great Mosque was begun in 785 and greatly extended under the rule of al-Hakam II (961–76). The palace was built in the 10th century for Adb al-Rahman III (ruled 912–61), who named it after his favorite wife. Al-Hakam II, who was a historian, also had one of the greatest libraries of the Islamic world, which contained 400,000 books indexed in forty-four catalogs.

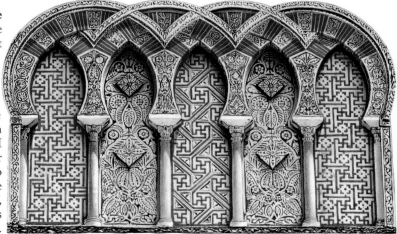

Industry

The Muslims enriched Spain in many ways. They improved farming with the introduction of irrigation and new crops, including cotton, sugar cane, and rice. They also developed new industries, among them pottery, paper making, sugar refining, and, most importantly, wool and silk cloth manufacturing. Precious fabrics, like the 12th-century silk fragment (see left), were in great demand in Europe, Northern Africa, and the Near East.

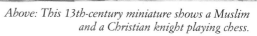

Above: This 13th-century miniature shows a Muslim and a Christian knight playing chess.

Powerful minister

Hisham II was just eleven years old when he became caliph in 976, and effective control was taken over by his prime minister, the Yemeni noble Abu Amir, known as al-Mansur. The new ruler began plundering churches in a series of campaigns against Christians. In 997, al-Mansur even took control of the important Christian pilgrimage site of Santiago de Compostela. In all, he led more than fifty campaigns against Christian strongholds.

Right: This stone relief from al-Mansur's palace shows a lion killing an antelope – a symbol of the triumph of Islam over its enemies.

Below: This decoration from an ivory casket shows Abd al-Malik, who succeeded his father al-Mansur and ruled from 1002 to 1008. He is flanked by two servants.

End of the caliphate

The Cordoba caliphate ended in chaos. Al-Mansur's sons succeeded him as ruling prime minister, while the real caliph remained without power. Civil war broke out, and Cordoba itself was sacked and burned by Berbers in 1013. Eighteen years later the last caliph, Hisham III, abdicated, and control passed to regional Muslim dynasties in cities such as Seville, Granada, Malaga, Toledo, and Zaragoza. The regional rulers constantly fought each other.

Arabic influence

During the 10th century, a large number of Andalusian Christians chose to convert to Islam. The remaining Christians gradually became Arabized in speech and dress. Some women began to put on a veil when they went out in public, and many Christians stopped eating pork. The local language took on many Arabic words, and some still remain in Spanish today. Christian scholars began writing in Arabic rather than Latin. The Christians of al-Andalus were later known as Mozarabs (from Arabic *musta'rib*, meaning "made an Arab").

Left: Almoravid clay seal.

The Almoravids

The Almoravids were Berbers from the western Sahara who had conquered much of northwestern Africa (see page 44). In 1085, their leader Yusuf ibn Tashfin was asked for help by the Andalusian Muslims after Alfonso VI, the King of Leon and Castile, had captured Toledo. The following year, Yusuf defeated Alfonso in battle, and the Almoravids went on to take control of al-Andalus and remained rulers until 1147. They ruled al-Andalus from their capital of Marrakech.

Averroes

The great philosopher and physician Ibn Rushd (1126–98), known in the West as Averroes, spent most of his life in Cordoba. He is famous for his works on Aristotle and Plato, and his commentaries influenced Christians and Jews as well as Muslims. He taught that religious faith and reason were different ways of arriving at the truth. Averroes was personal physician to the Almohad rulers, who ruled al-Andalus after the Almoravids.

Right: In this painting by Raphael, Averroes is shown in a white turban, standing behind Aristotle.

Left: The 12-sided Golden Tower of Seville was built by the Almohads to control the entry of ships into the city's harbor.

The Almohads

The Almohads came from the Masmuda tribe of Berbers. Under their ruler Ibn Tumart (c.1080–1130) they fought against the Almoravids in North Africa, attacking Marrakech in 1130. The Almohads crossed to al-Andalus in 1146 and soon took control of the Muslim province. After suffering a terrible defeat by Christian troops in 1212 and losing 10,000 men in battle, the Almohads withdrew to North Africa.

The Nasrids

Muhammad al-Ghalib, the first Nasrid ruler, entered into an alliance with the Christian king of Castile and created a small state based in Granada, attracting Muslim refugees from the reconquered Spanish territories. Although the Nasrid kingdom was relatively weak, its palace, the Alhambra (see page 41), is one of the finest pieces of Islamic architecture in Spain.

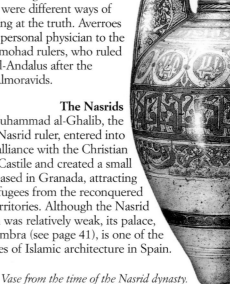

Vase from the time of the Nasrid dynasty.

The Fatimids

The Prophet Muhammad with his daughter Fatima and her husband Ali, Muhammad's cousin.

The Fatimids were a religious and political dynasty that ruled over Egypt and North Africa from the 10th to the 12th centuries. As followers of the Ismaili branch of Shi'ite Islam, their main aim was to oust the Abbasids and become the ruling force in the Muslim world. They tried to achieve this by military means and by the use of a vast missionary network. Though they never succeeded in their aim, their capital in Cairo became an important center of art and learning. From the second half of the 11th century, the dynasty suffered a gradual decline. Territories fell away, and before the end of the 12th century, the remaining lands became part of the Abbasid empire again.

A fountain pavilion in the courtyard of the Ibn Tulun Mosque, built at al-Qatai (Cairo) in 879.

The Ismailis

This Shi'ite sect was named after the son of the sixth imam ("spiritual successor") to the Prophet, Ismail ibn Jafar. Ismailis believed that Ismail should be the seventh imam, while other Shi'ites supported his younger brother. When Ismail died before his father, his followers believed that the son's descendants were the true successors. The Ismailis gained influence in present-day Iraq and Yemen in the 9th century and sent missionaries to other parts of the Islamic world. They wanted to overthrow the Sunni caliphate of the Abbasids, and at the beginning of the 10th century one of their followers founded the Fatimid dynasty.

The Tulunids

This dynasty of rulers was founded by Ahmad ibn Tulun (835–84), the son of a Turkish slave who grew up in the Abbasid capital of Samarra. In 869, Tulun became governor of Egypt and Syria, and after raising his own army, he was soon semi-independent of the Abbasids in a region surrounding the River Nile. He made his capital at al-Qatai (a district of present-day Cairo) and developed his region's agriculture and trade. His Tulunid successors did less well, however, and by 905 the region was back under full Abbasid control.

Gatehouse to the Fatimid capital of Mahdiya.

Fatimid founder

At the beginning of the 10th century, an Ismaili leader named Ubayd Allah went to Ifriqiya (present-day Tunisia) in North Africa. He claimed descent from the Prophet's daughter Fatima through Ismail's son Muhammad, making him the "hidden imam" for whom the Ismailis were waiting. In 909 he proclaimed himself al-Mahdi ("the Rightly Guided One"), built a new capital on the coast, called Mahdiya, and started to put together a large fleet of ships. He reigned until 934 as the first Fatimid caliph.

Sicily

Muslim Arabs had first crossed to the island of Sicily early in the 9th century. The Fatimids wasted no time in appointing a governor to the island, which formed a useful base for launching raids along the Mediterranean coast. The Fatimids had to deal with great opposition from Berbers and Sunni supporters of the Abbasid caliph, and the Byzantines wanted to regain power in Sicily. Eventually the island fell to the Normans, and Roger II became King of Sicily in 1130.

Silk ceremonial cloak made for King Roger II in the Sicilian court workshops in 1133. Craftsmen in the workshops were Muslims, and the cloak has an inscription in Arabic. It was later used as a coronation robe by Holy Roman Emperors.

The al-Azhar Mosque in Cairo quickly developed into a center of learning and became a university, as it still is today.

Conquest of Egypt

Wishing to expand to the east, the Fatimids sent their first expedition to Egypt in 913. After several more unsuccessful attempts, they finally conquered Egypt under caliph al-Muizz (ruled 953–75) and pressed on into Palestine and Syria. They set about building a new walled capital on the River Nile near Fustat, calling it al-Qahira (meaning "the victorious"), which in English became Cairo. The first major building there was the al-Azhar Mosque, named after Fatima az-Zahra (Fatima the Resplendent), the ancestress of the Fatimids.

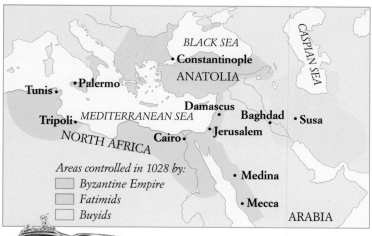

Areas controlled in 1028 by:
- Byzantine Empire
- Fatimids
- Buyids

Missionaries and merchants

The Fatimid caliphs set up a large network of missionaries, and they built libraries and colleges to train them. Their task was to convert people to Ismaili Shi'ism and get them to support the Fatimid cause. This meant working against the Sunnite order in the many lands controlled by the Abbasid caliphs, and so agents worked in secret under instructions from the chief missionary in Cairo. The Fatimids also developed trade around and through the Red Sea, providing an alternative route to the Persian Gulf (controlled by the Abbasids). Merchants helped to spread their beliefs.

Sea trade grew as the Fatimids controlled both coasts of the Red Sea.

Arts and crafts

Successful trade and farming meant that the court of the Fatimid caliphs was rich and ostentatious. This in turn caused a new enthusiasm in the decorative arts, which made Cairo the most important cultural center in the Islamic world. Expert artisans made wonderful ceramic and glass objects, including many that were carved from solid blocks of rock crystal. Carvers also used wood and ivory, and high-quality furniture made in Cairo was exported throughout the Mediterranean region.

Left: A rock-crystal ewer carved in Cairo.

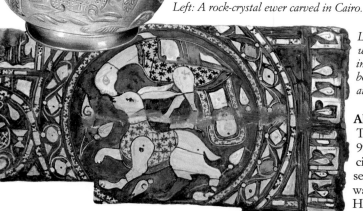

Left: This Fatimid wooden panel was inlaid with ivory and bone to show a hawk attacking a hare.

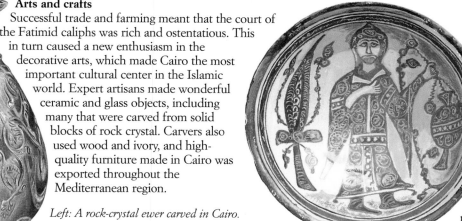

Above: This 11th-century Egyptian ceramic bowl, probably made by Muslims, shows a Christian priest.

Different beliefs

Apart from the reign of al-Hakim (see below), the Fatimid period was one of religious tolerance. The Fatimids' liberal attitude toward other beliefs came about by necessity, because many of the Muslims living in their lands remained faithful to Sunni Islam. This led them to appoint Christian and Jewish scholars as state officials, who ensured that their own people were allowed religious freedom.

Al-Hakim

The sixth Fatimid caliph, al-Hakim (ruled 996–1021), had a new mosque built outside the city walls. This was probably used to instruct selected students in Ismaili beliefs, while al-Azhar was meant for general Islamic education. Al-Hakim was an eccentric, extreme ruler, who persecuted non-Muslims and brought in laws banning dogs, chess, and the making of women's shoes. His reign ended mysteriously when he rode his favorite mule into the hills and was never seen again.

Left: Mihrab (niche which shows direction of Mecca), of the al-Hakim Mosque in Cairo, completed in 1013.

Above: This carved ivory plaque shows a Fatimid court dancer.

Decline

During the long reign (1036–94) of al-Mustansir, Fatimid provinces were lost to invaders and local dynasties, and there were struggles between Berber and Turkish groups in the army. Famine and plague made things worse, and further family splits occurred on the death of al-Mustansir. A Fatimid army was defeated by Christian crusaders in 1099, and in 1130 the caliph was murdered by members of an Ismaili sect called the Assassins. From then on, the Fatimid caliphs lived without great influence in Egypt.

Left: 11th-century illustration of Fatimid soldiers in ceremonial dress.

Saladin

In 1169 a Kurd by the name of Salah al-Din (or Saladin) was appointed vizier of Fatimid Egypt. He soon took total command of the region, and in 1171 he formally abolished the Fatimid caliphate and proclaimed a return to Sunnite Islam for Egypt. Saladin went on to unite all the Muslim territories of Egypt, northern Mesopotamia, Palestine, and Syria, as well as recapturing Jerusalem from the Christians in 1187.

Saladin (1137–93).

Founding Seljuq

During the 8th and 9th centuries, tribes of nomadic Turkish shepherds continued moving west from the steppes of central Asia. During the 10th century, a number of these tribes, called the Oghuz, settled near the Sry Darya river under their leader, Seljuq. Around 960 these tribes, who were later called Seljuks after their founding leader, adopted Islam.

Relief of a double-headed eagle from the city wall of the Seljuk capital of Konya, in present-day Turkey.

Mahmud of Ghazna listening to poetry. He was a patron of the arts as well as a warrior.

The Ghaznavids

The Ghaznavid dynasty was founded by Sebuktegin (ruled 977–98), a former Turkish slave who became a powerful military commander. Toward the end of the 10th century, Sebuktegin established his own independent principality and was recognized as governor of Ghazna (in modern Afghanistan). His son Mahmud (ruled 998–1030), who was a devout Muslim, expanded the Ghaznavid empire while paying homage to the Abbasid caliph in Baghdad. In 1026, Mahmud's powerful army, made up mainly of Turkish slaves and mercenaries, defeated the Seljuks.

The Seljuk Turks

The Seljuks were descended from a group of nomadic tribes from central Asia. They became Muslims in the 10th century and for three hundred years ruled an Islamic empire that stretched across Mesopotamia and the Middle East to the Asian part of modern Turkey. Their powerful sultans and viziers were responsible for many great Islamic buildings, but their empire split into separate princedoms. The Seljuk defeat of the Byzantines in the 11th century led to battles with Christian crusaders, but the sultanate that was left was not destroyed by them, but by Mongol invaders from the east.

Above: Mahmud launched many attacks into the plains of northern India. Here his forces are shown using a giant catapult, called a "mangonel," against a mud-brick fortress.

This precious gold painted ceramic bowl from Persia may represent a Seljuk ruler and his wife.

Tughril and Chaghri Beg

In 1038 Seljuq's grandsons, Tughril Beg (c.990–1063) and Chaghri Beg (c.990–1060), divided the Seljuk territory between them. The younger brother Chaghri controlled the northern region of Khorasan, while Tughril established himself at Nishapur (in present-day Iran) and looked to the west. In 1040, the Seljuks defeated the Ghaznavids at Dandanqan, and fifteen years later their forces took control of Baghdad. Tughril was given many honorary titles by the Abbasid caliph, who had power in name only.

The expanding Seljuk empire.

BLACK SEA
CASPIAN SEA
KHWARIZM
Uzgen
Amasya
Nicea
Ankara
Erzurum
Bukhara
Konya
Kayseri
Battle of Manzikert
KHORASAN
Samarkand
Antalya
Dandanqan
Balkh
MESOPOTAMIA
Sultanya
Gorgan
Nishapur
Damascus
Herat
Ghazna
Baghdad
Isfahan
ARABIA
Shiraz
RED SEA
Mecca
INDIAN OCEAN

Left: This Seljuk jug, dating from around 1200, shows a Chinese influence, reflecting the great extent of trade routes.

Above: Traders resting at a "caravanserai," or inn.

Developing trade

Seljuk army patrols provided security for traveling merchants, who traded meats, hides, and textiles produced by the tribespeople. During the 11th and 12th centuries, many caravanserais were built along trade routes, usually every thirty kilometers or so apart. These offered shelter for caravans and soon developed into trading centers. They were also built in towns, where they often contained workshops. These buildings led to a further increase in crafts and trade.

13th-century miniature of a Seljuk ruler on his throne.

Expanding empire

Tughril Beg was succeeded as Seljuk ruler by Chaghri's son Alp Arslan (ruled 1063–72). In 1071, Alp Arslan inflicted a devastating defeat on an enormous Byzantine army at Manzikert, capturing Emperor Romanus Diogenes. This important victory weakened Byzantine power and opened the way for Turkish tribespeople to settle in Anatolia, the Asian peninsula of modern Turkey. The next Seljuk leader, Malik Shah (ruled 1072–92), expanded the empire further east and south.

The Crusades

Under the leadership of Malik Shah, the Seljuks captured Jerusalem in 1072 and Damascus four years later. The Christian Byzantines, who had been hurt by the loss of Anatolia, were outraged by Muslim control of their Holy Land, and Emperor Alexius I Comnenus asked the Pope for help. The First Crusade (see page 28) was called in response to this appeal, and in 1097 the Seljuks were defeated by crusaders under Godfrey of Bouillon. Jerusalem was recaptured by the Christians two years later, and its Muslim inhabitants were slaughtered.

Pope Urban II gives his blessing to Christian knights about to set out on the First Crusade.

Young students listen to their teachers in a mosque school, while a servant operates a ceiling fan.

Madrasas and mosques

Seljuk vizier Nizam al-Mulk (1018–92) was responsible for organizing the empire during the reigns of both Alp Arslan and Malik Shah. The vizier had *madrasas* ("Islamic colleges") built in all important towns, so that the state's future religious scholars and administrators could be taught in a uniform way. Languages, literature, and science were taught in the madrasas, as well as theology and law. Many mosques were built by the sultans at this time, including the great Friday Mosque at Isfahan, which rose on the site of an earlier Abbasid building.

Left: This 13th-century vase shows scenes from the poet Firdawsi's Book of Kings.

The south vaulted hall of the Friday Mosque at Isfahan, which faces in the direction of prayer.

Detail from the façade of the Ince Minare madrasa in Konya, built in 1260.

Art and literature

Since the Seljuk Turks had very little written literature or Islamic cultural tradition, they adopted literary Persian as their language of art and culture. The greatest early poet was Abu al-Qasem Mansur (c.940–1020), known as Firdawsi, who wrote an epic poem of 60,000 verses called the Book of Kings. The finished poem was presented to Mahmud of Ghazna, who only later realized what a valuable work it was. During the 12th century, pottery flourished under the Seljuks in the Persian region, while important metalworking centers developed in Anatolia.

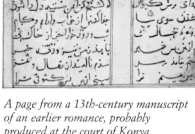

A page from a 13th-century manuscript of an earlier romance, probably produced at the court of Konya.

This bronze bucket from Herat is inscribed with the Islamic date Muharram 559 (1163 CE).

Divisions and decline

The empire was weakened by the Seljuks' practice of dividing their provinces among the ruler's sons. This created independent principalities which often fought against each other. In Persia, Tughril III tried to regain power but was killed in battle against Khwarizmian Turks in 1194. By the end of the 12th century, Seljuk power remained only in Anatolia – and that was not to last much longer.

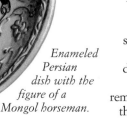

Enameled Persian dish with the figure of a Mongol horseman.

The Sultanate of Rum

Toward the end of the 11th century, the Anatolian Seljuks were hemmed in by crusaders and Byzantines. They formed a smaller state known as the Sultanate of Rum (the name referring to the eastern Roman Empire of the Byzantines). The sultanate's capital was established in Konya, but in 1243 Mongol warriors tore in from the east. They defeated the Seljuk ruler Kaikhosrau II, and all his lands had to pay tribute to the invaders. The remaining Seljuk rulers were merely figureheads, and the dynasty died out at the end of the 13th century.

Islamic Worship

Worship is an extremely important aspect of Islam, and praying forms one of the five special duties that all Muslims must perform. The traditional movements of the prayer ritual help Muslims devote themselves to worship, concentrating on Allah and thinking of nothing else. Muslims pray at home or in a mosque, where men and women usually pray in separate areas. On Fridays, men meet in a special congregation for their midday prayers. In Islamic countries, shops and businesses close at that time, and if a man does not attend for more than three weeks, he is thought to have left Islam.

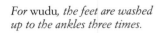

For wudu, *the feet are washed up to the ankles three times.*

Washing

Ritual washing, called *wudu*, is part of the discipline and preparation for prayer. This includes washing the hands, mouth, nostrils, face, arms, ears, neck, and feet. Washing should be done with running water, and this is available for people entering a mosque. If no water is available (as centuries ago in the desert), sand or earth may be used for a dry, symbolic wash.

1. Prayer begins by concentrating on Allah. While standing, worshipers place their right hand lightly over their left.

Prayer ritual

Salah, or "ritual prayer," is performed five times a day (see page 12). The times for *salah* are called by the *muezzin*, or proclaimer, but Muslims may also pray at home. There is a series of set movements for *salah*, which includes four basic positions. Muslims also say personal prayers, called *du'a*, in which they ask Allah for help or guidance.

A muezzin, calls Muslims to prayer from a minaret beside a mosque. This 16th-century miniature comes from India.

2. Worshipers bow, placing their hands on their knees. Showing respect and love for Allah, they recite three times, in Arabic: "Glory be to my great Lord, and praise be to Him."

4. Worshipers return to the kneeling position, sitting on their feet and placing their hands on their knees. There is a set number of the sequence for prayers at different times of the day.

3. Worshipers get down on their knees and prostrate themselves, touching the ground with their forehead and nose. They say three times: "Glory be to my God, the greatest of the great."

Prayer mats

The place where a Muslim prays must be clean. Worshipers do not have to use mats to kneel on, but some Muslims have favorite prayer mats that they keep at home. These may be made of wool, cotton, or straw. Prayer mats often have geometric patterns, or sometimes pictures of famous mosques, but they never show images of people. They often contain a deliberate mistake in the pattern to remind the owner that nothing except Allah is perfect.

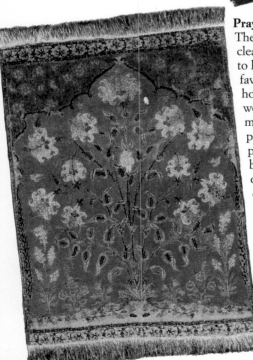

This prayer mat is made of wool and silk. It was woven in the 17th century, during the reign of the Mogul emperors in India.

This compass is used by worshipers to find the direction of Mecca.

Qibla

The *salah* must be said kneeling in the direction of the Kaaba in Mecca, known as the *qibla*. At first Muhammad had told his companions to turn toward Jerusalem when they prayed, but later he received a revelation to face Mecca. To determine the *qibla* when not in the Mosque, Muslims use a special compass, often incorporated in modern prayer mats.

Misbaha or subha are strings of prayer beads used by Muslims to praise Allah. They are normally composed of 99 beads, each one standing for one of the beautiful names of Allah. Muslims believe that repeating God's names over and over brings them closer to him.

Left: Muhammad preaching from a wooden minbar in his mosque in Medina. While Muhammad preached from the top step, the imam is only allowed to stand on the second step.

Attending a mosque

The word *mosque* comes from the Arabic *masjid*, which means "place of prostration." The first mosque was built by Muhammad and his followers after his arrival in Medina. A mosque does not have to be a special building – any clean space will do. Mosques are places for communal prayer, and they also act as centers of Muslim social life, especially in non-Islamic countries. There is often a *madrasa*, or school, attached to the mosque.

The Ottoman sultans had special furnishings made for their mosques. This walnut box was made in the early 16th century to hold thirty manuscript volumes of the Qur'an.

Inside the mosque

Inside a mosque, the prayer hall is spacious and airy. There are no chairs, but carpets are often marked out with lines so that worshipers know where to stand, kneel, and sit. Mosques have no pictures or statues, and they are decorated with patterns and words from the Qur'an. A niche or alcove, called a mihrab (above), is set in the wall opposite the entrance. Sometimes this is in the shape of a shell, and when worshipers face this, they know they are facing toward Mecca. To the right is a minbar, or pulpit, where sermons are delivered.

Minaret

Mihrab

Prayer hall

Minbar

This imam is using a megaphone to lead an outdoors communal prayer.

Courtyard

Fountain for wudu

The *imam*

There are no priests in Islam. The communal prayers are led by a prayer leader, called an imam, who is chosen by the congregation. Any respected Muslim who is well-trained in the prayer can become an imam. In general, he is the most learned and most respected person in the assembly. If the mosque does not have an imam, any adult male may lead the prayers. When Muslims gather in the mosque for Friday prayer, the imam gives a sermon from the minbar.

The Crusades

For a period of two hundred years, from the end of the 11th to the end of the 13th centuries, Christian popes and kings mounted fierce military attacks against Muslim rulers in the Middle East. Their expeditions became known later as "Crusades," since they were made on behalf of the Christian cross. The First Crusade was called in response to an appeal to the Pope by the Byzantine emperor for help against the Seljuk Turks. The appeal came at just the right time, as there was a general wish among the rulers of Europe to counter Muslim power, which they saw as a threat. The Crusades may have slowed the advance of Islam, but by the 13th century the Muslims were more concerned about the invading Mongols.

Pope Urban II (c.1042–99) thought that a military Crusade would help unite Christian knights and nobles.

The First Crusade
Pope Urban II called for the First Crusade at the Council of Clermont in 1095, giving a rousing speech against Islam. Three years later, the crusaders took the cities of Edessa and Antioch, and in 1099 they captured Jerusalem, which had been in Muslim hands for 460 years. They showed no mercy to Jerusalem's Muslim and Jewish inhabitants, slaughtering all they could find.

Right: A Christian map of Jerusalem, which was seen as the center of the Holy Land and one of the main goals of the Crusades.

Left: In 1098, the crusaders took Antioch (in present-day Turkey) after a seven-month siege.

Below: The routes across land and sea of the eight Crusades.

Warriors of the cross
The knights and ordinary soldiers who took up arms to fight far from their homeland called Muslims a race of "infidels," or faithless people. The Crusaders saw themselves as warriors of the cross, fighting for the right of a Christian king to rule the Holy Land where Jesus had lived and died. Yet many probably joined the Crusades more with a sense of adventure than out of religious ideals. These men were mainly looking for the chance to win fame and fortune.

The Crusader states
Following the capture of Jerusalem, the Crusaders gained control of a narrow strip of land along the eastern Mediterranean coast. They set up four states – the Kingdom of Jerusalem, Principality of Antioch, and Counties of Edessa and Tripoli (see the map left) – and put them under the control of Christian rulers. They wanted other Europeans to come and settle in these states, but the few who came did so mainly as pilgrims.

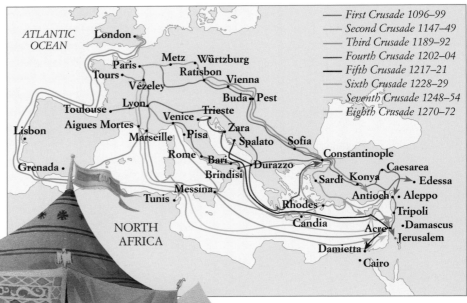

First Crusade 1096–99
Second Crusade 1147–49
Third Crusade 1189–92
Fourth Crusade 1202–04
Fifth Crusade 1217–21
Sixth Crusade 1228–29
Seventh Crusade 1248–54
Eighth Crusade 1270–72

The Islamic response
In 1144, a Turkish regional governor named Zangi (1084–1146) recaptured Edessa from the Crusaders. This earned him the title "victorious king" from the Abbasid caliph, but the loss of Edessa brought about the Second Crusade. Then in 1187, the great Muslim leader Saladin (1137–93) defeated the Crusaders at the Battle of Hattin and recaptured Jerusalem. This led in turn to the Third Crusade, which failed to recover Jerusalem but helped protect the Crusader states.

This illustration shows a Crusader surrendering to Saladin, at Hattin.

The Fourth Crusade

The Fourth Crusade, called by Pope Innocent III, was meant to attack Egypt, but the Crusaders never got there. Instead, they agreed to help the powerful Venetians attack the city of Constantinople, the capital of the Byzantine Empire. The Crusaders succeeded in capturing the city, sacking it, and then setting up a so-called Latin Empire, which lasted until 1261. This furthered the disagreements and distrust between the Western Roman Catholic and Eastern Orthodox Churches.

Later Crusades

Later expeditions did not give the Crusaders any great success. The Fifth Crusade took the Egyptian port of Damietta but failed to reach Cairo. Holy Roman Emperor Frederick II led the Sixth Crusade and managed to become recognized as ruler of Jerusalem in 1229, but the Muslims regained the city 15 years later. The Seventh Crusade repeated the Fifth, while the Eighth was aimed at Tunis, in North Africa, but ended as another costly failure.

Right: During the Seventh Crusade its leader, King Louis IX of France, was captured by the Egyptians. Here the king is shown facing his captors, who released him only on payment of a huge ransom.

Left: A map of medieval Constantinople (ancient Byzantium, modern Istanbul).

Below: Krak des Chevaliers was built on the site of an older Islamic fortress. It was captured by Muslim forces in 1271.

Crusader castles

In the 12th century, the Crusaders began building fortresses to keep routes open and to protect land they had conquered. They placed the castles at strategic locations. Krak des Chevaliers (French-Arabic for "castle of the knights"), in modern Syria, was built to protect a route to and from the Mediterranean Sea. The strongest of the Crusader castles, it could hold a garrison of 2,000 soldiers and enough food for five years.

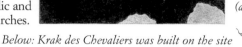

A Templar knight goes into battle.

Military religious orders

During the period of the Crusades, certain orders of monks took on a military role, such as the Order of the Hospital of St. John of Jerusalem, known as the Hospitalers. The Poor Knights of Christ and the Temple of Solomon, or Templars, also fought to protect pilgrims and others. At the end of the 12th century, both orders moved to Acre, but there was always distrust between them.

Other Crusades

During the Crusader period, Christian armies were trying to drive the Moors from Spain. In 1212, Alfonso VIII of Castile won a great victory over forces of the Muslim Almohad caliph at Navas de Tolosa in southern Spain. In the very same year, an army of Christian boys and girls gathered in France and set off for Palestine in a "Children's Crusade." Many died on the way and none reached their goal.

Right: In the battle at Navas de Tolosa the Spanish captured the caliph's banner.

Left: Some crusader knights used the crossbow, which fired further than an ordinary bow but took much longer to load.

Weapons

A Christian knight's arms included a sword, lance, mace, and axe. Muslim warriors fought with sabres, heavy lances, lightweight javelins, and pear-shaped maces. Cavalry formed the main striking force of Muslim armies, and their small Arab horses were quicker and more maneuverable than the Crusaders' large warhorses. The favorite Muslim weapon was the bow and arrow, and each cavalryman had a quiver filled with light, deadly arrows.

End of the Crusades

Louis IX of France led the Eighth Crusade but died of plague in Tunis in 1270. Ten years earlier, the slave force known as the Mamelukes (see pages 32–33) had defeated the invading Mongols in Palestine and extended their rule to Syria. In 1291, the Mamelukes turned their attention to what remained of the crusader states. In 1291 they captured Acre and drove the crusaders out of Palestine for good.

A Mameluke horseman wields his heavy sword.

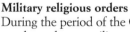

Mongols and Timurids

The Mongols were originally groups of nomadic tribes scattered across the grasslands of central Asia. Early in the 13th century, they were united under a single leader, Ghengis Khan, who set about creating a vast empire. Before long, the Great Khanate of Ghengis had three offshoots – the Golden Horde, the Chagatai, and the Ilkhanate (see the map below). Many Mongols in the west of the empire adopted Islam, and they were reunited under a Muslim ruler, Timur, who came to power in the 14th century. He and his descendants in the Timurid dynasty ruled until 1506, exactly 300 years after Ghengis Khan set out to conquer the world.

Ghengis Khan (c.1167–1227).

This Mongol helmet was made in China for a high-ranking officer.

Founding ruler

In 1206, a man named Temujin, a chieftain's son who had already proved himself in war, united the nomadic Mongol tribes. At a great assembly, he was proclaimed Ghengis Khan (meaning "universal ruler") because the Mongols believed that he would conquer and rule the whole world. He soon set about creating an empire, first making attacks on the northwestern border of China. Then, in 1218, Ghengis turned west and headed toward the lands of Islam.

Mongol animal spirits.

Mongol warriors were expert bowmen. They could shoot accurately even when their horses were galloping at full speed.

Expert horsemen

The Mongols herded sheep and goats, for which they needed their most prized possessions – horses. They showed great skill in breeding, training, and riding their short, stocky horses. Boys and girls learned to ride as soon as they could walk. Mongol armies took huge numbers of horses with them so that every warrior could have a fresh mount whenever he needed it.

Charging into battle, Mongol warriors attack the enemy with maces, lances, and swords.

Spirit worship

Ghengis Khan and his people worshiped many spirits, and every clan had its own animal spirit – the founding ruler's was the legendary Blue Wolf. They believed that sacred spirits lived in fire, wind, and running water. The most important spirit was the "Eternal Blue Sky," which controlled all the forces of good and evil. Some men, called shamans (Mongolian for "those who know"), were thought to be able to communicate with the supernatural world of spirits. When Ghengis Khan became ruler, Mongol shamans said that he was the earthly representative of the Eternal Blue Sky.

Warfare

Mongol cavalry columns traveled far apart, communicating with flags and smoke signals. Warriors were well-equipped with a wide range of weapons, backed up by giant crossbows and siege engines such as mangonels. Ox-drawn carts carried equipment and food, engineers built and repaired bridges, and women collected arrows and killed wounded enemy.

Right: Hulagu (1217–65), grandson of Ghengis Khan, and the first Ilkhan ruler. His brothers, Mongke Khan and Kublai Khan, were also Mongol rulers.

From Bukhara to Baghdad

In 1218 Ghengis Khan was outraged when Mongol envoys were executed in the Muslim shahdom of Khwarizm. He rode at the head of more than 100,000 men, totally destroying the fortified cities of Bukhara, Samarkand, and Nishapur, and killing millions of people. After Ghengis returned to the Chinese front and died there, his grandson Hulagu continued westward. In 1258, Hulagu's forces besieged and then captured Baghdad, killing all Muslims including the Abbasid caliph.

The extent of the Mongol Empire in 1280.

KHANATE OF THE GOLDEN HORDE

CHAGATAI KHANATE

• Karakorum

Bukhara • • Samarkand

THE GREAT KHANATE

Aleppo •
Nishapur • • Herat
Baghdad ILKHANATE

• Beijing

TIBET

• Ningxia

ARABIA

PACIFIC OCEAN

Ghengis Khan leaves the mosque at Bukhara, where he is said to have told the people: "If you had not committed great sins, God would not have sent a punishment like me upon you."

The Ilkhanate

The Persian lands south of the Caspian Sea, from Baghdad in the west to Balkh (in present-day Afghanistan) in the east, came under the rule of Hulagu. He took the title *Ilkhan* (or "subordinate khan") and pledged support to the Great Khan, his brother Mongke. Thirty years after Hulagu's death, his great-grandson Ghazan (ruled 1295–1304) converted to Islam and broke close ties with the other Mongol khans. Ghazan's successors ruled over a successful Muslim state until 1335.

Tiles from a summer palace built for a late 13th-century Ilkhan in Iran.

Timur

Timur (or Tamerlane, 1336–1405) was born near Samarkand and grew up in the Chagatai Khanate. Since he walked with a limp, he was known as Timur-i-Lenk, or Timur the Lame. Many of the people to the west of the Khanate had become Muslims. Timur, who was born into a Mongol-Turkic tribe of Tatars and claimed to be a descendant of Ghengis Khan, was a well-educated, devout Muslim. He first took control of the Transoxiana region of the Khanate, and made Samarkand his capital.

Timur's name appears on this silver coin from the late 14th century.

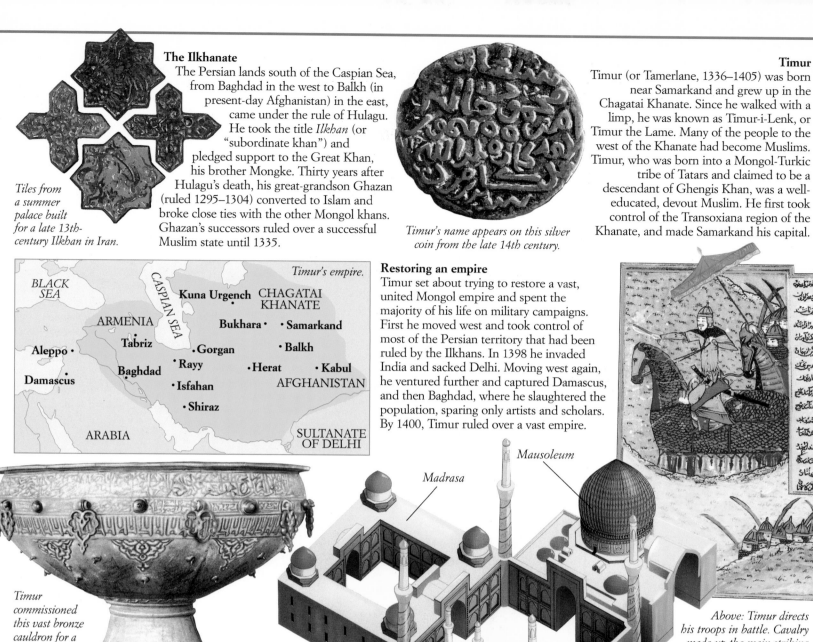

Restoring an empire

Timur set about trying to restore a vast, united Mongol empire and spent the majority of his life on military campaigns. First he moved west and took control of most of the Persian territory that had been ruled by the Ilkhans. In 1398 he invaded India and sacked Delhi. Moving west again, he ventured further and captured Damascus, and then Baghdad, where he slaughtered the population, sparing only artists and scholars. By 1400, Timur ruled over a vast empire.

Madrasa

Mausoleum

Sufi hospice

Above: Timur directs his troops in battle. Cavalry made up the main striking force of his army, backed up by infantrymen.

Below: Detail of a miniature painted in Timurid Herat around 1495.

Above: The Gur-i Mir mausoleum in Samarkand, where Timur and his descendants were buried.

Timur commissioned this vast bronze cauldron for a Sufi shrine in 1399.

Samarkand

Though Timur spent most of his time away, he did his best to make Samarkand a worthy capital city. In 1399, he imported master builders from all over his empire, and work began on the vast Bibi Khanum Mosque, which was later ruined by earthquakes. This and other buildings were covered in beautiful blue and gold mosaics. Timur also built a wonderful mausoleum for his favorite grandson, where his own body was taken after he died on a campaigning expedition to China in 1405.

Timur with three of his sons.

This ewer of white jade was made under the Timurids.

The Timurid dynasty

After his death, Timur's territories were divided between his two surviving sons. After years of rivalry between them and other descendants, the youngest son – Shah Rukh – reunited many of the lands and ruled from Herat until 1447. He founded a library in his capital, which became a center of learning and the arts in the Persian tradition. Schools of miniature painting, as well as wood and jade carving, flourished under the Timurids. The dynasty's last ruler, a great-grandson of Timur, was defeated by the Shaybanids in 1506 (see page 37). Another descendant, Babur, was governor of Ferghana and went on to found the Mughal Empire (see page 38).

Origins

The Mamelukes were slave soldiers. They got their name from the Arabic *mamluk*, meaning "one who is owned" (or "slave") and were first used in the 9th century by the Abbasid caliph al-Mutasim, in Baghdad. The slaves were neither Arabs nor Muslims, but Turks who were highly trained in military skills and given Islamic instruction. They soon became an important part of Muslim armies and spread throughout the Islamic world.

The Ayyubids

Having overthrown the Fatimids in 1171 (see page 23) and founded the Ayyubid dynasty, the Kurdish commander Saladin used slaves to fight in his army. His Ayyubid successors imported Kipchak Turks from the northern shores of the Black Sea, and in 1250 the Mamelukes helped the Ayyubids to defeat the Seventh Crusade led by Louis IX. However, the Mameluke commander Baybars then led a group of officers who murdered the Ayyubid sultan. They replaced him with the first Mameluke sultan of Egypt.

A page from a military manual. Four young Mameluke horsemen ride around a square pool. They learned to read and write Arabic as part of their training.

This ceramic bowl, dating from around 1200, shows an Ayyubid prince.

The Mamelukes

By the 13th century, the Mamelukes had formed dynasties both in Egypt and in India. Having helped Islam against Christian Crusaders, the Mamelukes under Turkish leadership then defeated the invading Mongols in Palestine and Syria, where they extended their rule. They brought about a golden age of Islamic art and architecture. With Cairo as their splendid capital, they also made Damascus a worthy provincial city. Under later Circassian leaders, the Mamelukes declined and came into conflict with the Ottomans, who conquered Egypt and Syria in 1517. Though they no longer had their own empire, the Mamelukes remained as local governors under Ottoman rule.

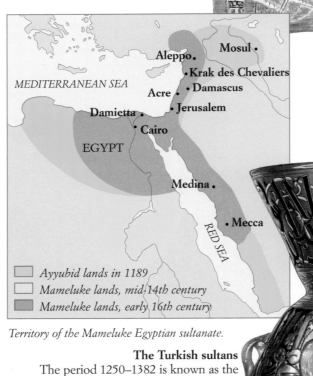

Above: In 1288, under their sultan Qalawun, the Mameluke cavalry charged in and recaptured the crusader outpost of Tripoli, in present-day Lebanon.

The Sultanate of Delhi

In India, the assassination of Mahmud of Ghur in 1206 allowed a Mameluke officer, Qutb al-Din Aibak, to become sultan. This led to a series of "slave sultans" who reigned until 1290, when the Khaljis took over. The Sultanate of Delhi was to last until 1526, when it was defeated by Babur (see page 38). During this time, the sultans made great use of slave soldiers to expand their territory in the Indian subcontinent.

Sultan Qutb al-Din Aibak had this huge sandstone "Tower of Victory" built in Delhi as a minaret beside the mosque known as the "Might of Islam."

Map:

Aleppo•

Mosul

•Krak des Chevaliers

MEDITERRANEAN SEA

Acre• •Damascus

Damietta• •Jerusalem

•Cairo

EGYPT

Medina•

•Mecca

RED SEA

☐ Ayyubid lands in 1189
☐ Mameluke lands, mid-14th century
☐ Mameluke lands, early 16th century

Territory of the Mameluke Egyptian sultanate.

The Turkish sultans

The period 1250–1382 is known as the Turkish period of Mameluke rule. At this time, they were led by a succession of Kipchak Turks (also called Bahris), and it was a period of great success and expansion. Having fought off the Christian Crusaders and the invading Mongols, the Mamelukes earned the thanks of all Muslims. They also made an Abbasid prince caliph of Cairo (under the control of their own sultan) and supported local rulers in Mecca and Medina.

The expanding state

Baybars, who ruled as sultan of Egypt from 1260 to 1277, was one of the most outstanding of the Mameluke sultans. He was also a strict Muslim. He strengthened the military position of the Mamelukes by rebuilding all the Syrian citadels that had been destroyed by the Mongols and commissioning new arsenals and warships. During the long reign of al Malik an-Nasir (ruled 1293–1341), the Mamelukes made peace with the Mongols and overcame famine to maintain the prosperity of Egypt.

This early 14th-century mosque lamp from Cairo is inscribed with the name of Sultan al Malik an-Nasir.

Left: Men drinking in a tavern. Taverns were usually run by Christians, but later Mamelukes enforced the Islamic ban on alcohol.

Right: Fishermen illustrated in a 14th-century Mameluke miniature.

Below: Master metalworker al-Zain made this brass basin, inlaid with gold and silver, in Syria in the late 13th century.

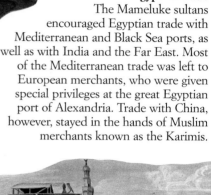

Non-Muslims

When the Mamelukes came to power, they showed tolerance towards their Jewish and Christian subjects, as the Ayyubids had done. Over the years, however, this situation changed. Islamic religious leaders condemned Christian practices, and ordinary Muslim citizens resented the fact that Christians held high positions in Egypt. In 1301, the Mamelukes ordered all Christian churches in Egypt to be closed, and more and more non-Muslims converted to Islam.

Toward the end of the Circassian period, the Portuguese were competing for Indian trade. This illustration shows a Portuguese attack on Muslim merchants.

Egyptian trade

The Mameluke sultans encouraged Egyptian trade with Mediterranean and Black Sea ports, as well as with India and the Far East. Most of the Mediterranean trade was left to European merchants, who were given special privileges at the great Egyptian port of Alexandria. Trade with China, however, stayed in the hands of Muslim merchants known as the Karimis.

The Circassian sultans

The years 1382–1517 are called the Circassian period of Mameluke rule. At this time, the Mamelukes were led by a succession of Circassians from the northwestern Caucasus (between the Black and Caspian Seas), also called Burjis. From the time of the first Circassian sultan, Barquq (ruled 1382–99), however, the empire went into decline. By 1400, the Mamelukes had lost such power that the Timurids were able to overrun Syria.

Above: Venetian trade ambassadors are received by the governor of Damascus, the administrative capital of Mameluke Syria.

Books

Historical writing was very important to the Mamelukes, who produced huge chronicles, bibliographical dictionaries, and encyclopedias. Even non-Muslim scholars wrote in Arabic, since it was the language of the ruling class. There was great competition between the cities of Cairo and Damascus, where beautiful copies of the Qur'an were made and other literary works were decorated with colorful miniature paintings.

Below: Miniature from a 13th-century Syrian manuscript of stories about a clever man of the world.

Left: In this miniature from a manuscript of the Fables of Bidpai, the king of the hares gives an audience to his subjects.

Below: The decorated dome of the mausoleum of Sultan Qaitbay, built in Cairo in 1474. The dome shows two patterns intertwined – a geometric star pattern and a floral arabesque.

Mausoleums

The Mamelukes were responsible for many religious buildings, including mosques and *mastabas* (tombs with sloping sides and flat roofs), but they are best known for their magnificent mausoleums, especially in Cairo. These were richly decorated with carved stone and ornamental masonry. Baybars was the only Mameluke sultan to be buried in Damascus, in a mausoleum decorated with a frieze of golden mosaics.

Science and technology

A 13th-century illustration of the ancient Greek philosopher and scientist Aristotle. He was known to Muslims as the "first teacher."

Early Muslim scientists were greatly influenced by the works of ancient scholars. They translated many old manuscripts, especially those of the great Greek philosophers and scientists. The efforts they made were useful to the whole world, since without them many ancient texts might have been lost during the European Middle Ages. Arabic became the leading language of science, and Muslim scientific output was large and wide-ranging. The 11th-century scientist al-Biruni, for example, wrote more than 150 works, on subjects ranging from astronomy and mathematics to history and philosophy. It was usual for Islamic scientists to carry out research in several subjects, constantly questioning the theories of earlier scientists and testing their own results. In this way, they gained knowledge and, they believed, a greater understanding of Allah.

A beautifully inscribed page of an old Qur'an, which was always at the heart of Islamic knowledge.

A variety of influences

Several Greek works had been translated first into Syriac (the language of ancient Syria), and Muslims used these as sources, as well as Pahlavi and Sanskrit texts, ancient languages of Persia and of India. Knowledge of astronomy had been passed on by Parsees and Sabaeans, and there was much mathematical knowledge to be gained from the Hindus of India. The ancient Chinese had made great technological discoveries, and these were also studied.

Above: Muslims adopted the Hindu number system, using nine digits and a zero. These were known as "Indian numerals," but when they were later brought to Europe, they were called Arabic.

Right: A page from al-Khwarizmi's book, parts of which were later translated into Latin. This introduced algebra to Europe.

The Greek inheritance

It is said that Aristotle appeared to the Abbasid caliph al-Ma'mun (786–833) in a dream. Perhaps it was this that persuaded the caliph to have the great philosopher's works translated into Arabic. In fact, translation of ancient Greek works had begun under the Umayyads, but during al-Ma'mun's reign the famous library in Baghdad became a center of translation and an institute of science.

Mathematics

Great developments were also made in mathematics. Muslims used Babylonian and Indian sources for their work in arithmetic, and their knowledge of geometry was based on the Greek mathematicians Euclid and Archimedes. In the 9th century, a Persian mathematician named Muhammad al-Khwarizmi (c.800–50) wrote a book in Arabic, the title of which meant "the science of restoring and balancing." This work was on algebra, and the word itself comes from the Arabic word "restoring" in the title – *al-jabr*.

Left: Muslim doctors treated most patients with herbs and drugs, using surgery only when necessary. This illustration shows a Caesarean operation to deliver a baby.

Medicine

Basic medical knowledge was gained from the ancient Greek physician Galen. The first hospital was opened in Baghdad at the beginning of the 9th century. A Persian named Muhammad al-Razi (known as Rhazes, 865–923) studied anatomy, recorded diseases such as smallpox and measles, and wrote an enormous encyclopedia of medicine.

Left: A later copy of a 9th-century work on optics by Hunayn ibn Ishaq, who clearly understood the anatomy of the human eye.

Below: A 13th-century illustration of a pharmacist preparing drugs.

A page from an 11th-century Arabic translation of Dioscorides.

Optics

Muslims based their early scientific study of light and sight on the work of Galen, which was useful but misleading. In the 11th century, the mathematician and scientist Ibn al-Haytham (known as Alhazen, c.965–1040), who came from Basra in modern Iraq, transformed the subject. He showed that rays of light from the sun are reflected off things around us and then enter our eyes.

Botany

The first Muslim studies of plants and their medicinal properties were based on work by the ancient Greek physician Dioscorides, who had described nearly 600 plants. His lists were translated in the 9th century, while at the same time the Persian botanist Abu al-Dinawari (c.815–95) compiled his own *Book of Plants*. Three centuries later, Muslim botanists put together a dictionary of herbal medicines that was more comprehensive than any other such work in the world.

Engineering

Building on the work of Archimedes, Muslim scientists made great strides in practical engineering and technology. They were particularly interested in the design, construction, and use of machines. Among the most popular and useful were water-raising machines, which were used along with dams and canals for irrigation projects. Around 1200, an engineer named al-Jazari invented a range of machines, including water-clocks and fountains. He described them in his *Book of Ingenious Mechanical Devices.*

Above: This device, called a "gnomon," was used to find the direction of Mecca and determine the times of prayer from the position of the sun.

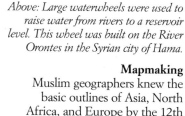

Above: Large waterwheels were used to raise water from rivers to a reservoir level. This wheel was built on the River Orontes in the Syrian city of Hama.

Astronomy

The early Muslims were expert astronomers. They drew on the knowledge of Persian and Indian scholars, as well as the Greek astronomer Ptolemy. They inherited from Ptolemy a belief that it was essential to keep testing and checking their own observations and theories. Following careful observations made in Baghdad and Damascus, Muslim astronomers completely rewrote their set of astronomical tables in the early 9th century. They also developed astronomical instruments such as the astrolabe, which helped with navigation.

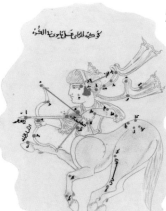

Above: The constellation Sagittarius, from the 10th-century Book of Fixed Stars. *Knowledge of the stars was also useful to Muslim astrologers in their attempts to foretell the future. Many astronomers served as astrologers at court (see below), which meant that their scientific findings were taken more seriously.*

Right: Since there were no telescopes before the 17th century, Muslims used other astronomical instruments. This large wooden device is called an "armillary sphere." In it, the hoops represent circles on the sphere of the heavens such as the orbits of the moon and planets. While three astronomers look along the hoops, probably at a star, another adjusts the central ring with a plumb line, while a fifth records the results.

Mapmaking

Muslim geographers knew the basic outlines of Asia, North Africa, and Europe by the 12th century. A Moroccan geographer named al-Idrisi (c.1100–66) had already traveled widely before he was asked by the Norman king of Sicily, Roger II, to produce a map of the world. It proved to be very accurate for its day.

Right: Like most early Islamic examples, al-Idrisi's map puts south at the top.

Right: A 13th-century miniature of a library in Baghdad.

Libraries and learning

Since Muslim scholars translated so many texts, and many wrote their own new works, libraries soon grew up to house them. These quickly became institutions of learning, where students could take in all this new knowledge. A great library was built in Baghdad early in the 9th century. Around 970, the al-Azhar mosque was founded in Cairo, and its school grew into a university with free tuition. This was probably the world's first university.

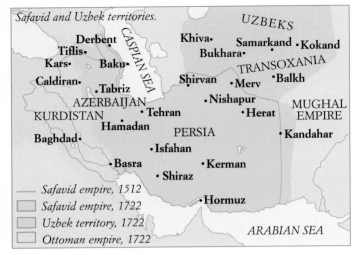

Safavid and Uzbek territories.

UZBEKS

Derbent • — Khiva • — Samarkand • • Kokand
Tiflis • — Bukhara •
Kars • — Baku • — TRANSOXANIA
Caldiran • — Shirvan • • Merv • • Balkh
• Tabriz • • Nishapur
AZERBAIJAN
KURDISTAN — • Tehran • • Herat — MUGHAL EMPIRE
Hamadan •
Baghdad • — PERSIA — • Kandahar
• Isfahan
• Basra — • Kerman
• Shiraz

— Safavid empire, 1512
☐ Safavid empire, 1722
☐ Uzbek territory, 1722
☐ Ottoman empire, 1722

• Hormuz

ARABIAN SEA

The Safavids

The Safavids were descended from the founder of the Safawiyah order of Sufi dervishes, Safi od-Din (1252–1334), who gave them their name. Their rule was established in 1501 when Ismail I (1486–1524) captured the city of Tabriz and was made shah of Azerbaijan, reintroducing the pre-Islamic title of shah for the first time in hundreds of years. In the following year, he became shah of Persia.

This 16th-century Persian miniature shows the prophet Muhammad, Ali (see page 14), and Ali's sons Hasan and Husayn. The picture represents Shi'a Islam crossing the sea of eternity.

Safavids and Uzbeks

The Safavids and the Uzbeks shared much of their history during the 16th and 17th centuries, having met in battle for the first time in 1510. Their territories bordered on each other (stretching across lands previously under Timurid control), and hostilities were heightened by the fact that the Uzbeks were Sunnite Muslims, whereas the Safavids were Shi'ites. The Safavids expanded throughout Persia and beyond, until their empire collapsed in the early 18th century. The Uzbeks, who were a loose federation of tribes and never achieved an empire, eventually fell to the Russians. The Safavid territory roughly covers modern Iran, while the Uzbek lands form present-day Uzbekistan.

Shi'ite state

Ismail I claimed descent from the seventh of the twelve principal imams (early leaders) acknowledged after the death of Muhammad by the Shi'ite branch called "Twelvers." The shah declared Shi'ism to be the state religion throughout the new Safavid Empire. Shi'ite scholars came from Arabia, Iraq, and Syria, and state-appointed religious leaders helped the shah introduce strict Shi'ite rules.

Ismail I stabs an Ottoman cavalryman with his sword at the Battle of Caldiran, where the Safavid forces were defeated in 1514.

War on two fronts

In order to expand beyond their Persian borders, the Safavids had to contend with the Uzbeks in the northeast and the Ottomans to the west. Though Ismail won initial victories over the Uzbeks, he suffered a serious defeat by Ottoman sultan Selim I in 1514. The Safavids lost territory in Kurdistan and Baghdad, and the empire weakened further during the reign of Ismail's son Tahmasp.

Capital at Isfahan

The greatest Safavid ruler, Abbas I (1557–1629) known as "the Great," became shah in 1588. In the early years of his reign, Abbas established his empire's capital in Isfahan. There he laid out a completely new city, building bridges, gardens, and impressive structures such as the Lutfallah and Shah mosques. The heart of the beautiful city was a rectangular public square known as the "Design of the World."

Above: The complex Khwaju Bridge was built across the River Zayandeh at Isfahan in 1650. It had a road for caravans and two tiers of pedestrian arcades.

A decorated helmet made for Abbas the Great.

Left: Abbas the Great receiving a commercial legation in his palace at Isfahan.

Persian art

Under the Safavid rulers, and Abbas the Great especially, Persian art was given new life. Isfahan was further developed by Abbas II (ruled 1642–66) and included wonderful garden palaces. Many workshops were set up in the capital, and the tradition of Persian carpet-weaving was revived under royal patronage. Religious poetry was encouraged, and ceramics concentrated on showing scenes in beautiful settings.

Below: This early 17th-century ceramic tile shows an idyllic garden scene.

Persian economy

Under Abbas the Great, the Safavids developed business relationships with the European powers as well as the Mughals of India, improving diplomatic relations with the court of the Russian tsars. At the same time, the shah encouraged Christian and Jewish merchants and craftworkers to come to Isfahan, and he was tolerant of their different beliefs and customs. In order to make trade easier, a single imperial coinage was created.

New troops

In 1599, Abbas the Great decided to change the way in which his army was formed. He created three new bodies of troops, made up of artillerymen, musketeers, and slaves. The new system worked. In 1603, the Safavid army defeated the Ottomans and went on to take Baghdad. Abbas also expelled Portuguese traders who had seized Hormuz in the Persian Gulf.

Ousting rivals

Abbas the Great did his best to make sure that the religious leaders of his empire did not have any great influence on the commercial workings of the state. They had great power in other ways, however. The shah gave funds for the upkeep of Shi'ite shrines, founded teaching colleges, and provided religious leaders with income from landed estates. Sunnite rivals were harshly treated, Sufi shrines were destroyed, and brotherhoods banned.

A Sufi saint and fakir listen to the music of a lute player. Sufism was suppressed under the Safavids.

The Uzbeks

The Uzbeks were a group of about thirty Turkic-Mongol tribes who took their name from an early 14th-century khan (or leader) of the Golden Horde (see page 30). Uzbek (or Öz Beg) converted to Islam in 1313, and in the 1330s began building a new capital for the Golden Horde, called New Saray, north of the Caspian Sea. The name Uzbeks came to be used for all the Sunnite Muslims who formed the ruling class of the Golden Horde. Their capital was later destroyed by Timur (see page 31).

Head from a statue of Timur (c.1336–1405).

The Shaybanids

Muhammad Shaybani was defeated and killed by the Safavids at the Battle of Merv in 1510, but he had set up an Uzbek Shaybanid dynasty that would last for the whole of the 16th century. The Shaybanids ruled from their new capital of Bukhara, where they built impressive mosques and bridges. The last Shaybanid ruler, Abd Allah II (reigned 1558–98) led military campaigns to try to increase Uzbek territory.

Right: Babur enters Samarkand in 1500. He was soon driven out again.

Abd Allah II.

This madrasa and mosque were built at Registan Square in Samarkand in 1646.

Three khanates

During the 16th and 17th centuries, wonderful buildings were constructed and decorated in the cities of Samarkand and Bukhara. After the Shaybanids were replaced by other dynasties, however, the Uzbek federation began to split up. In the 17th century, it divided into separate khanates (regions ruled by a khan), called Bukhara (which included Samarkand), Khiva (to the northwest), and Kokand (in the Fergana valley). By the 19th century, all three khanates had been invaded and captured by Russia.

Safavid decline

After the death of Abbas the Great, the Ottomans soon recovered most of the lands they had lost. The empire was in decline, and the shah's authority was gradually being lost to religious scholars who demanded more say in the running of the state. In 1722, after a seven-month siege in which more than 80,000 citizens died, Shah Husayn was forced to surrender Isfahan to invading Afghans.

Muhammad Baqir Majlisi (1627–98) was the leading Shi'ite scholar of his day.

Tribal federation

Early in the 15th century, a descendant of Ghengis Khan, Abul-Khayr (1411–68), became leader of the Uzbeks at the age of 17. During Abul-Khayr's rule, the tribes came closer together and formed a federation. They moved southeast, toward the city of Samarkand, Timur's former capital. Abul-Khayr was killed by invading Dzungars, but in 1495 the federation conquered areas of Transoxania (modern Uzbekistan). Abul-Khayr's grandson, Muhammad Shaybani (reigned 1500–10) drove Babur (see page 38) out of Samarkand, and the tribes occupied this and other major cities. The Timurid dynasty fell to Shaybani in 1506.

Bukhara was a famous trading center. Covered bazaars filled with stalls and workshops were devoted to different crafts and business activities. Three of its domed markets have survived to this day.

Babur was proud of his Mongol descent. This miniature shows him being given the crown of India by Timur, who in reality died 121 years before Babur's reign began.

Mughal Empire

Akbar the Great.

The Mughals (or Moguls) took their name from their ancestors, the Mongols (see pages 30–31), who had adopted Islam. They came south from central Asia in the early 16th century and established a Muslim dynasty which ruled an increasingly large empire in the Indian subcontinent. The early Mughal emperors, all direct descendants of the founding ruler Babur, were tolerant of other religions. The culture of the Hindu majority was allowed to co-exist with that of Islam. When this situation changed in the 17th century, the Mughals lost the support of their subjects, opposition grew from many sides, and the empire rapidly declined.

The founding emperor

Babur (1483–1530), the warrior ruler who founded the Mughal dynasty, was directly descended from Timur on his father's side and from Genghis Khan on his mother's side. He became ruler of Ferghana (in present-day Uzbekistan) but failed to conquer Samarkand, Timur's former capital. After capturing Kabul (in Afghanistan), he invaded north India, and in 1526 his army of 25,000 men defeated the sultan of Delhi's much larger force at Panipat.

Early expansion

After he entered Delhi, Babur was declared emperor of Hindustan and his name was read out in the Grand Mosque. The new ruler had to win two more great victories to make his empire safe. In 1527, his army defeated the Rajput clans and then a group of chiefs who had served the sultan of Delhi. But Babur was more than a great warrior. He wrote poetry in Persian and kept diaries that became a memoir of his life. He also created luxurious gardens in all the cities he conquered.

Left: Akbar's private audience hall in the palace complex at Fatehpur Sikri.

Above: A 16th-century Indian painting shows Mughal warriors chasing the sultan of Delhi's fleeing army.

Establishing rule

Babur was succeeded by his son, Humayun (1508–56), who invaded Gujarat in 1535. In the 1540s, however, the emperor was forced to take refuge in Persia by the Afghan Surs, and he only managed to reclaim Delhi in 1555. The following year, Humayun was killed when he fell from the roof of his library, and he was succeeded by his 13-year-old son Akbar (1542–1605). This young man was to become the greatest ruler of the Mughal Empire, which he also extended in Gujarat and Bengal (see map on page 39).

A Mughal court scene.

Life at court

In 1571 Akbar began building his capital at Fatehpur Sikri, near Agra. There he set up new court routines. In the morning, he would hold meetings in a public audience chamber, where he dealt with everyday affairs of state with his ministers and military generals. In the afternoon and evening, he received dignitaries, artists, and other important people in his private audience hall. The emperor also liked listening to music and watching spectacles, including elephant fights.

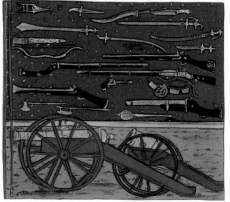

Governing the empire

Akbar was a wise ruler. He defeated the Hindu Rajputs and then won their support and strengthened the alliance by marrying several Rajput princesses. Akbar also introduced a new system of administration, appointing ministers to help him and dividing the empire into twelve provinces, each with its own governor and separate tax collector. He built new roads to help trade and reformed the empire's money system.

Left: Akbar was a great military leader. In a chronicle of his reign, he had a whole chapter devoted to weapons.

Religious tolerance

Knowing that it would be difficult to rule his empire without the support of Hindus, Akbar did not force them to become Muslims. He restricted the power of the Islamic religious leaders, stopped the collection of taxes at Hindu holy places, and then abolished the special tax that non-Muslims had previously had to pay. He listened to people of all religions and received Portuguese Christians from Goa.

Above: Portuguese Jesuit Father Monserrate visited Akbar's court and tried to convert him to Christianity.

Jahangir and Jahan

Jahangir (1569–1627) inherited a powerful empire when he succeeded his father, Akbar. Though he expanded it further, Jahangir preferred life at court to commanding his armies. Unlike his father, he loved reading. On his death, he was succeeded by his own son, Khurram, who fought off other family members to become the next emperor, Shah Jahan. He was a strong leader who was willing to take tough decisions, such as the destruction of Hindu temples in order to gain the support of Muslim religious leaders.

Left: Shah Jahan shown in all his glory.

Below: This jade and ruby pen box comes from the time of Shah Jahan. It contains a knife to cut the pen, a stylus handle, and a spoon for mixing ink.

Floral decoration

In the 16th century there was a trend in Mughal art toward illustrating plants more realistically. This continued into the 17th century, especially under Shah Jahan, when flowering plant designs were used to decorate all sorts of objects. Shah Jahan was himself a calligrapher and took a great interest in art, especially the decoration of books.

Mughal daggers with ornamental hilts and scabbards.

Monumental architecture

Akbar's first major architectural project was the building of a tomb for his father, Humayun, in Delhi. The magnificent building was surrounded by a large garden crossed by water channels. In turn, Akbar's own tomb, at Sikandara, was set in a vast garden complex. This monumental architecture led finally to the building of the world's most famous mausoleum, the Taj Mahal (see page 41), built by Shah Jahan for his wife.

Below: Humayun's tomb took nine years to build and was completed in 1571.

The last Great Mughal

Aurangzeb (1618–1707), son of Shah Jahan and the sixth emperor, was the last of the so-called Great Mughals. He imprisoned his father and killed two of his brothers to gain the throne, moved the capital to Delhi, and became a ruthless ruler. During his forty-nine year reign, he conquered several states in southern India. At the same time, Aurangzeb followed strict Islamic policies, making enemies of his Hindu subjects and in this way weakening the empire.

Above: Aurangzeb reading the Qur'an.

Below: The spread of the Mughal Empire (1526–1707).

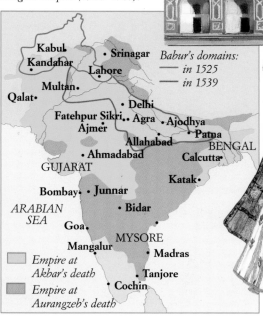

Babur's domains:
— *in 1525*
— *in 1539*

Empire at Akbar's death

Empire at Aurangzeb's death

Right: A mechanical toy of a tiger attacking a British soldier. It was made for the sultan of the Muslim state of Mysore.

Marathas Opposition

The chiefs of the Marathas, a Hindu people from western India, were united by Sivaji and they made him their king in 1647. Ten years later, the Marathas began fighting the Mughals for territory and expanded their kingdom. After Sivaji's death, the ministers who succeeded him found it difficult to hold their federation together.

Left: Sivaji (1627–80), warrior chief and founder of the Maratha kingdom.

Decline of the Empire

The Mughal Empire was in decline before Aurangzeb's death. The long wars against the Marathas put great strain on the Mughal treasury and standards of government declined. The Persians sacked Delhi in 1739, and from then on the major powers in India were the Marathas and the British East India Company, which gained Bengal in 1765. The last Mughal emperor, Bahadur Shah II, was exiled to Rangoon in 1857.

Art and architecture

Through the centuries, Islamic art has widened and been influenced by different traditions in various parts of the world. There have been great achievements in all aspects of art and architecture. In the visual arts, much of the work is based on geometric designs rather than images of living things, including humans. This is especially true of religious works and comes from the view that if artists created living images, they would be imitating Allah. Earlier religious authorities also feared that people might worship idols, which is forbidden by the Qur'an. In architecture, different Islamic empires such as the Moors, Mughals, and Ottomans, produced great works in their own distinctive styles.

The inscription on the base of this ceramic mosque lamp dates it at 1549. The lamp was painted in black cobalt and turquoise before the glaze was applied.

Decorative arts

Islamic religious authorities always frowned on the use of precious, expensive materials for decorated objects. Muslim artists and craftsmen were nevertheless skilled at creating beautiful objects. Metalworkers mainly used bronze and brass, sometimes inlaid with gold, copper, or silver. Potters engraved or painted ceramics before using glazes of many colors, later adding a metallic pigment to make outstanding lusterware. The nomadic herders of western Asia had a long tradition of using wool to make carpets, and their Muslim descendants developed this art with great skill.

Above: This 14th-century carpet shows four stylized animals. A century later, carpets like this were being sold to Europe.

Left: This Mameluke perfume sprinkler is made of brass inlaid with silver and gold designs and inscriptions.

Left: The style of decoration on this 13th-century ivory casket from Arabic Sicily is very similar to Islamic metalwork of the same period.

Design motifs

Since there has always been a restriction on images of living things, artists developed a very distinctive use of geometric designs. These designs were used on a variety of materials so that a motif that was originally developed for textiles, for example, might then be used on pottery or glassware. Four main styles of decoration developed in time: calligraphic, arabesque, geometric, and floral. Arabesque is a form of ornamentation made up of a pattern of winding stems and stylized leaves.

Detail of a wooden Qur'an stand from the 13th century, richly carved with geometric and floral designs.

An early 17th-century illustration in the style of the Mughals, rulers of northern India, who were masters of color.

Left: This detail from a 17th-century fresco comes from a palace at Isfahan where the Safavids entertained their European guests.

Illustrated books

Poets and storytellers played an important part in ancient Arabian and Persian society, and their works were respected by the early Muslims. In later centuries, calligraphers and painters inscribed and decorated manuscripts and books. Like other artists, writers and illustrators were supported by rulers and other wealthy people. They all had a very strong sense of color. The poet Nezami (c.1141–1217), for example, based a classic poem on the seven traditional Persian colors of red, yellow, green, blue, black, white, and sandalwood.

Painting

Figurative art was disapproved of by Muslim theologians. Despite this, Muslim monarchs often commissioned figurative paintings in the confines of their palaces, away from the public eye. The Safavids and Mughals were passionate patrons of painting. The Safavid ruler Shah Tahmasp (1524-76) spent two decades finding the best painters to bring to his court. In addition, Western painting gradually came to influence Islamic art through trade and diplomatic ties.

Left: In this beautifully decorated page, the Naskhi script appears in the form of a bird.

Right: This beautiful mosaic of the sun watching a lion chasing a deer appears above a madrasa door in Samarkand.

Calligraphy

The importance of writing is stressed in the Qur'an, and calligraphy – the art of beautiful writing – has always been considered the highest form of art by Muslims. Calligraphers were held in honor because they inscribed the Qur'an on parchment or paper, and they soon came to show their skill on other materials, such as tiles and coins. Arabic letters, which read from right to left, were written in several scripts. The Kufic script, from the town of Kufah south of Baghdad, was used by early Muslim calligraphers. Six classic styles were later codified: Thuluth, Naskhi, Muhaqqaq, Raihani, Tawqi, and Riqa.

The early 15th-century mosaic details above and right come from Persia and central Asia.

Mosaics

Glazed ceramic tiles have been used throughout the centuries to decorate the walls of Islamic buildings. Very often the richly colored tiles are arranged in geometric patterns, or mosaics. The individual tiles may be of varying sizes, but none are very large. The walls of many of the oldest and most recent Islamic structures, including the Dome of the Rock (below left), are covered in beautiful blue tiles.

Below: View of the Alhambra palace in Granada, Spain. The fortified palace was built by the Nasrid rulers in the 13th century in their own typical style.

Architecture

The first mosques were very simple buildings, but through the centuries they have developed in different ways in various parts of the Islamic world. The main feature of Persian and Turkish mosques became a large dome, while in North Africa and Spain they were covered with beautiful tiles. Most major buildings, including palaces and mausoleums, were designed with elaborate arches and pillars, as well as domes. The roof of the Great Mosque in Cordoba was designed to be supported by more than a thousand pillars made of granite and marble. Modern Islamic architecture is based on the traditional styles.

Left: The Dome of the Rock, in Jerusalem, is covered in tiled panels.

Wondrous buildings

The Dome of the Rock, built in 692, is the first great monument of Islamic architecture and one of Islam's holiest shrines. Its dome rises 30 meters above the rock from which Muhammad ascended to heaven. The Selimiye Mosque is perhaps the greatest Ottoman building. It was designed by the famous court architect Sinan and completed in 1574. Many people consider the Taj Mahal to be the most beautiful building in the world. It was built by 20,000 workmen in 1631–53 for the Mughal emperor Shah Jahan as a mausoleum for his wife.

Left: The Taj Mahal in Agra, India, is made of polished white marble, with black inlaid decoration.

Above: The Selimiye Mosque in Edirne, Turkey, has 19 domes. Its four slender minarets are almost 71 meters high.

Ottoman Empire

In the 16th century, the Muslim Ottomans controlled one of the most powerful empires in the world. It had begun around the year 1300, when nomadic tribes migrated from central Asia to Anatolia. They soon conquered much of what is now European Turkey, taking Constantinople in 1453. The Ottomans' empire reached its peak under Sultan Suleiman the Magnificent. It began to decline after Suleiman's reign, however, gradually losing most of its European lands. Nevertheless, the empire held out until 1922, when the last sultan was deposed and its remaining territory became the republic of Turkey.

Osman, founder of the empire.

Origins

The Ottomans were named after Osman (c.1258–1326), known in Arabic as Uthman. Osman was chief of a nomadic Turkic tribe that had fled from the Mongols and settled in northwestern Anatolia. He led his Muslim tribe in fighting the Christian Byzantines, and in 1326 his son and successor Orhan (c.1288–1360) captured the important Byzantine town of Bursa and made it the Ottoman capital.

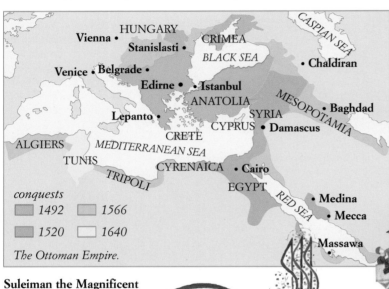

The Ottoman Empire.

conquests
- 1492
- 1520
- 1566
- 1640

Expanding empire

Orhan's son Murad (c.1326–89) captured Byzantium's second city, Edirne, in 1361. Less than a century later, Sultan Mehmed II (ruled 1451–81) captured the biggest prize of all when he took Constantinople. The Ottomans renamed the city Istanbul and made it the new capital of their empire. In 1517, Sultan Selim I almost doubled the size of the empire when he defeated the Mamelukes and gained control of Egypt, Palestine, and Syria.

Selim I (ruled 1512–20) was known as "the Grim." In order to get rid of rivals, he had his brothers and four of his sons murdered.

Suleiman the Magnificent

Selim was succeeded by his son Suleiman I (1494–1566), who became known in the Western world as "the Magnificent." But the Ottomans called him "the Lawgiver" because he revised the empire's legal system. Suleiman was an extremely able soldier and administrator, and Ottoman art and literature flourished during his reign.

The Ottoman navy fought an indecisive battle against the Venetians off southern Greece in 1499.

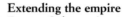

Suleiman's ceremonial signature.

Left: The brilliant Roxelana, Suleiman's favorite wife, was originally a slave from the Ukraine. She had a strong influence over Suleiman.

Extending the empire

During Suleiman's reign, the Ottoman forces captured Belgrade, and in 1522 they took Rhodes from the Hospitaler Christian knights. In 1526, the Ottomans defeated the Hungarians at Mohacs, and three years later they besieged but failed to take Vienna. Baghdad was captured from the Persians in 1534, and Suleiman then set about rebuilding the city.

Left: Suleiman attacked the fortress city of Belgrade in 1521.

The Janissaries

The Janissaries (so called from the Turkish for "new troops") made up a highly trained infantry force. They were originally made up of young Christian prisoners of war from the Balkans. The captives were given a Muslim education and taught to speak Turkish. The Janissaries (shown right, in a marching band) became known for their great discipline and acted as the sultan's bodyguards.

Army and navy

The Ottoman army's great strength lay in its cavalrymen, who fought in return for income from lands granted to them. Suleiman's army was made up of about 45,000 men, and mercenaries were added when required. The Ottomans also built up a large naval fleet, which ruled the Mediterranean. In 1571, it contained 230 ships, and though the Ottomans lost the Battle of Lepanto and most of their ships in that year, they rebuilt the fleet almost immediately.

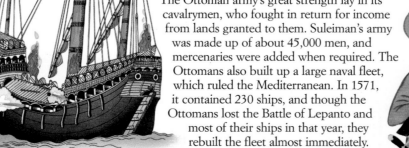

Architecture

Throughout the Ottomans' rule, mosques were built in abundance. The early mosques were traditional pillared buildings such as those in Bursa and Edirne. After the conquest of Istanbul, the city was renovated, and many mosque complexes were built. The most common feature was the design of domes to cover large floor spaces. The greatest Ottoman architect was Sinan (1489–1588), who helped design seventy-nine mosques, thirty-four palaces, and nineteen tombs.

The Bayazid Cami mosque complex in Istanbul was completed in 1506.

Military music

Ottoman military bands were first formed in the 14th century, and in later times they performed on ceremonial occasions. Favorite instruments were woodwind shawms (similar to the oboe), trumpets, drums, cymbals, and percussion sticks. The illustration above comes from a manuscript describing the events of Murad III's reign (1574–95).

Books and luxury goods

In the late 15th century, an imperial court studio was set up at the Topkapi Palace in Istanbul. By the time Suleiman I came to the throne, it had forty-one painters, as well as bookbinders and many other artists. Historical works honoring various sultans' reigns were designed, containing beautiful colored miniatures. The studio also became famous for designing luxury goods, from clothing and carpets to metalwork and jewelery.

Right: This early 17th-century gold necklace comes from Fez, in Morocco, which traded heavily with the western part of the Ottoman empire.

Trade routes

Busy overland trade routes ran through Ottoman territory, all the way across North Africa to the eastern fringes of the empire. In the 16th century, the Ottomans also gained control of sea routes through the Red Sea and Persian Gulf. Ships carrying spices from India and the Far East docked at the Ottoman-held ports of Aden and Jedda, from where they were taken overland to Anatolia.

A 16th-century parade helmet.

Center of the empire

The Ottoman court was based at the Topkapi Palace in Istanbul, which served as the center of government. As the former Byzantine capital was rebuilt and extended, successive sultans added mosques, hospitals, and libraries. As the population grew, so did the number of schools. They were ranked in a strict system: at the top were those founded by the current sultan, followed by those of earlier sultans, and then those founded by government officials and religious leaders.

This 16th-century silk caftan has a typical floral design.

Failed reforms

At the end of the 18th century, Sultan Selim III (right), who ruled from 1789 to 1807, tried to reform the Ottoman military system by replacing the Janissaries. The attempt failed, the sultan was overthrown, and most of the reform leaders were killed. Later reforms of taxation, property, and religious freedom met with opposition, and in 1865 people were calling for a constitutional government.

Above: Suleiman I receives his chief admiral, Khayr ad-Din, at the Topkapi Palace in 1533. Also known as Barbarossa (or Redbeard), the Turkish admiral was a former pirate.

The Crimean War

When Russia demanded the right to protect Orthodox Christians in the Ottoman Empire and moved south, the Ottomans declared war. They were joined by France and Britain against the Russians in the Crimean War of 1853–56. Conditions in the Crimea were appalling, and disease spread rapidly. Both armies were poorly led, and each lost more than a quarter of a million men. The Russians finally accepted peace terms.

Left: Ottoman soldiers during the Crimean War.

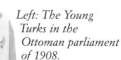

Left: The Young Turks in the Ottoman parliament of 1908.

The last sultan

In 1908, a group of revolutionary military officers called the Young Turks overthrew Sultan Abdul Hamid II. Twelve years later, a treaty stripped the empire of all its regions outside Turkey. In 1922, the last sultan, Mehmed VI, was forced to stand down, and in the following year Turkey was declared a republic.

Africa

Muslims began conquering the Mediterranean coastal strip of northern Africa in the 7th century. They soon reached the Atlantic Ocean in the west, converting Berber tribes on their way. Moving south across the Sahara Desert, they traded with the kingdoms that flourished in western Africa. At the same time Muslim merchants made their way down the coast of East Africa. The conquerors, traders, and settlers took their religious and cultural traditions with them. Today, Islam is still the dominant faith in North Africa, stretching from Mauritania in the west to Somalia in the east.

A decoration from the wooden minbar *(pulpit) of the Great Mosque of Kairouan, in present-day Tunisia.*

The Tuareg are a nomadic Berber people. Some continue to herd their livestock around the fringes of the Sahara Desert.

The Berbers traditionally carry silver daggers as symbols of dignity.

Islam arrives

Muslims began spreading from the Arabian peninsula into Africa in 640, just eight years after the death of Muhammad. Moving on from Heliopolis, they established a military settlement at al-Fustat, where 330 years later Cairo would be built. In 642, the port of Alexandria fell to Arab forces, and by the following year they had moved hundreds of miles along the Mediterranean coast to Barqa, in modern Libya. In 698, the Muslims took the ancient city of Carthage.

Berbers

The Berbers were the native inhabitants of the northern coastal strip of Africa that is known as the Maghreb. When the Arabs arrived in the 7th century, many Berber tribes resisted them at first. But by 702, they had mostly converted to Islam, as the Maghreb became part of the Umayyad caliphate run from Damascus. In 711, the Berbers were an important part of the Muslim force that crossed to the Iberian peninsula (see page 20).

Almoravids

The Arabic name of the Almoravids, al-Murabitun, means "men of the fortified monastery." They were Saharan Berbers who founded their community in the 1040s in northwestern Africa. In 1062, their greatest leader, Yusuf ibn Tashfin (ruled 1060–1106), made their capital at Marrakech, in modern Morocco. During Yusuf's reign the Almoravids took Tangiers and Algiers, and helped the Andalusian Muslims in Spain. In 1098, Yusuf adopted the title "Ruler of the Muslims."

Right: This Almoravid domed building was constructed over a well in Marrakech and was probably used for ritual washing.

Almohads

The Almohads, who came from the Masmuda tribe of Berbers, attacked the Almoravid capital at Marrakech, in 1130. Seventeen years later they captured the city, by which time they had also gained power in Muslim Spain. The Almohads insisted that their subjects convert to Islam, and under their leader Abd al-Mumin (ruled 1133–63), they unified the whole Maghreb region. They finally fell to Marinid Berbers in 1269.

Sunni Ali, leader of the Songhai, who disappeared mysteriously in 1492. He may have drowned in a flood.

Right: Minaret from the Kutubya, the principal mosque of Marrakech, spiritual and admistrative center of the Almohad dynasty.

Mansa Musa receiving an Arab trader.

Below: Sufism reached Timbuktu from the Maghreb in the 15th century. This book of prayers compiled by the Moroccan Sufi mystic al-Jazuli was used by a local religious brotherhood there.

Mali empire

Muslim traders traveled south and made the hazardous journey across the Sahara with caravans of camels, trading salt and luxury goods for ivory and gold. In the 13th century, the ruler of the Mali Empire, Sundiata Keita (reigned 1240–55), built cities on the trans-Saharan trade routes. Sundiata converted to Islam, and his successor Mansa Musa (ruled 1307–32) went on a pilgrimage to Mecca, accompanied by a baggage train of eighty camels laden with gold. Though the Mali ruling class were Muslims, many of their subjects continued to worship local African gods.

Songhai Empire

The Songhai people had already adopted Islam when their leader Sunni Ali (ruled 1464–92) attacked the Mali Empire. By 1475, he had captured Timbuktu and Djenné, and these trading cities became centers of Muslim learning. His successor, Askia Muhammad (ruled 1493–1538), further encouraged Islam among his people. The Songhai Empire was finally invaded by a Moroccan army in 1591.

Left: This small copy of the Qur'an was made around 1700. It is written in a distinctive African form of Arabic script.

South from the Horn

From around 1000, Arab merchants moved southward down the Indian Ocean coast from the Horn of Africa (modern Somalia), taking Islam to the city-states that had already been founded by local peoples. The Muslims traveled from Mogadishu and Mombasa to the great port of Kilwa. Cemetery remains on the island of Madagascar show that Muslim traders had arrived there by the 13th century.

Right: Rich farmland beside the River Nile.

A marabout shrine on the shore at Safi, in Morocco. It marks the burial place of a local Muslim saint.

Right: Students used to memorize verses from the Qur'an written on wooden tablets. This practice is still followed in West Africa today.

Historical scholarship

The level of scholarship in Muslim North Africa was high. The historian Ibn Khaldun was born in Tunis in 1332, and his *Universal History* forms a monumental study of the world's civilizations. He believed and showed in this work that civilizations rise and fall in cycles. Ibn Khaldun served as an ambassador to Timur before dying in Cairo in 1406.

Agriculture

Along with their Arabic language and Islamic way of life, Muslim traders and settlers took new crops and farming techniques to Africa. Sugar cane, melons, and varieties of rice were brought from southern Asia first to the Middle East and then to Africa. In this way, the range of African crops widened, and the Arab and Berber influence meant that livestock were moved around according to the seasons.

Below: This glazed ceramic container was used to serve warm soups and stews. It was made in Fez in the 18th century.

Decorative arts

The Maghreb's arts and crafts were greatly influenced by Berber traditions, such as unglazed pottery and heavy golden jewelry. The Arabic influence was felt more in the cities of Fez, Marrakech, and Rabat, where craft techniques became much more refined and colorful mosaic tiles decorated walls in vast geometric patterns. Wood carvers produced beautiful doors, shutters, and storage chests.

Mud-brick architecture

From as early as the 14th century, sun-dried mud bricks were used in Africa to build mosques. The bricks were placed around a wooden framework, which could also be used as scaffolding when repairs were needed after heavy rainfall. Two of the most famous examples are in the Mali cities of Djenné and Mopti.

MAGHREB

Tangier • • Tunis
Safi • • Fès Algiers
• Marrakech • Tripoli • Alexandria
• Cairo

• Mecca

• Timbuktu
• Djenné
MALI • Kano **ADAL** • Harer **SOMALIA**

Ottoman Empire, 17th century
Extent of Islam, 17th century
Songhai Empire, around 1515
Kanem-Bornu Empire, around 1600
— Trade routes
• Center of Muslim learning

• Kilwa
ATLANTIC OCEAN
Mozambique •

MADAGASCAR

Below: The Grand Malam is the leader of the Kanimbo people of northern Chad.

Left: The Great Mosque in Djenné was rebuilt in 1906 on the ruins of an original 14th-century building.

Modern times

The French army captured Algiers in 1830, and though the colonizers met fierce resistance from Muslim hill tribes, Algeria became part of France in 1871. Soon the rest of North Africa was colonized by the French, British, and Italians. Independence was regained in the 20th century, and today most of the countries of the northern half of the continent have Muslim majorities. The continent's largest Muslim populations live in Egypt, Nigeria, and Algeria.

Left: Algerian patriot Abd al-Qadir surrenders to the French governor-general in 1847.

Festivals

Muslims celebrate two important festivals – the Feast of Sacrifice and the end of the Ramadan fast – as well as others relating to events in the life of Muhammad. The festivals fall on particular days in the Islamic lunar calendar, which is made up of twelve months and is eleven days shorter than the Western solar calendar. This means that the festival dates do not follow the seasons and change each year in relation to Western dates. Each Islamic month begins when the first slender crescent of a new moon is sighted. Apart from the major festivals, others vary around the world according to Muslim traditions that have been handed down through the centuries.

Diagram of the Islamic (or Hijri) calendar and how it relates in 1424 AH to 2003–04 CE in the Western (or Gregorian) calendar.

1424

2003

MUHARRAM · SAFAR · RABI'I · RABI'II · JUMADA I · JUMADA II · RAJAB · SHA'BAN · RAMADAN · SHAWWAL · DHU'L-QA'DA · DHU'L-HIJJAH

JANUARY · FEBRUARY · MARCH · APRIL · MAY · JUNE · JULY · AUGUST · SEPTEMBER · OCTOBER · NOVEMBER · DECEMBER

Muharram

Muharram is the first month in the Islamic calendar, and so New Year's Day is celebrated when the new moon appears. This day also commemorates the very beginning of the calendar, which dates from the Hijra, when Muhammad went to Medina (see page 11). The first year was therefore 1 AH (meaning anno Hegirae or "in the year of the Hijra"). Though it is not a particularly important festival, Muharram 1 is celebrated by Muslims, who make a fresh start with new-year resolutions.

Above: Special sermons may be given during the important Islamic festivals.

Right: A Bianou dancer.

The Prophet's birthday

Mawlid al-Nabi, the Prophet's birthday, is celebrated on 12 Rabi al-Awwal (the third month). Some believe that this was also the day on which Muhammad died. On this day, parents tell their children stories of the Prophet's life and teachings. In some parts of the world, processions are also held.

Left: Kenyan girls celebrate Muhammad's birthday by reciting the Qur'an.

Bianou

The festival of Bianou is celebrated in the ancient African oasis town of Agadez, in Niger. This has been a stopping place for Saharan travelers, including nomadic Tuareg herdsmen, for centuries. Bianou celebrates the Hijra and involves two groups of Tuareg men who parade to the sultan's palace and the home of the imam of Agadez. Thousands of musicians and dancers join the procession, beginning the new year with a festival that lasts for three days.

Ashura

This special day takes place on the 10th of Muharram. It was traditionally a day of fasting before the time of the Prophet, and Muhammad fasted on this day. Some Muslims fast during the day and have a special meal at night. Ashura is especially important to Shi'ite Muslims, as it marks the day when Muhammad's grandson Husayn, called the Prince of Martyrs, was murdered (see page 15). Some men beat themselves with chains, to share Husayn's suffering. Special plays called tazias ("consolations") portray the events.

Right: This detail from a modern print symbolizes the massacre of Husayn. He is represented by the hand holding a sword, and the rose represents his martyrdom.

An Indian tazia float made for Ashura.

Laylat al-Miraj

On the 27th of Rajab, Muslims celebrate Muhammad's Night Journey (see page 11) by telling the story of the Prophet's ascension to the seven heavens. Muslims also remember that this was when Muhammad was told that Muslims should pray five times a day. The Prophet was first told to pray fifty times a day, but this was reduced to allow for people's weaknesses. Many Muslims spend this special night reading the Qur'an and praying, and in some countries mosques are lit up.

In this Ottoman miniature, Muhammad is surrounded by angels as he contemplates Allah.

Laylat al-Barat

On the night of the full moon before the start of Ramadan (on the 15th of the month of Sha'ban), Muhammad used to prepare for the fast by spending the first of many whole nights in prayer. Today, many Muslims do the same. They may also visit the graves of dead relatives and pray for their souls. Some believe that Allah determines everyone's fate for the coming year at this time. Traditionally sweets are made, and loaves of bread are given to the poor.

Laylat al-Barat is a time for prayer.

The Night of Power

Laylat al-Qadr is the Night of Power, when the Prophet received his first revelation (see page 10). This night is described in the Qur'an as "better than a thousand months." It is traditionally celebrated on the 27th of Ramadan, but since the date is not known for certain, some Muslims celebrate all the last five odd-numbered nights of Ramadan in the same way. Many spend the night of the 27th in prayer at the mosque.

An Ottoman miniature of Muhammad at the first revelation on Mount Hira.

Breaking the fast

Id al-Fitr celebrates the breaking of the month-long Ramadan fast and is known as the minor of the two great Islamic festivals (the other being the Feast of Sacrifice). It begins at the sighting of the new moon and so at the same time marks the start of the month of Shawwal. Most people rely on an official sighting, which is announced on radio and television in Muslim countries. Children receive sweets and other gifts, special cards are sent, and some families hang decorations up at home. It is a time of great joy, and people do not forget to make special offerings to the poor.

This greetings card wishes a "Happy festival."

This Muslim Chinese family is eating a special meal to celebrate the end of the Ramadan fast.

Id al-Adha

This Feast of Sacrifice is the most important festival in the Islamic year. It takes place on the 10th of Dhu'l-Hijjah and commemorates the special sacrifice made by Ibrahim (see above). It lasts four days, and everyone thinks about the pilgrims who have gone on hajj (see pages 56–57), for whom this is a very special occasion. Sheep and goats are sacrificed, and some families have their feast animals killed at a licensed butcher or slaughterhouse. The meat is shared among family, friends, and the poor.

Left: An angel stopped Ibrahim from sacrificing his son, and a ram was killed instead.

Right: Mu'in al-Din's marble tomb in Ajmer.

At Id al-Adha, a sacrificed camel can be shared by seven households.

Urs

At Ajmer, in northern India, Muslims hold a special festival during the first six days of Rajab. This is to commemorate the death of Mu'in al-Din, a Sufi who brought his Chishti brotherhood to India and died there in 1236. During the festival of Urs, thousands of pilgrims come to Ajmer. The town is decorated with lights and festoons, and a special dessert of rice and milk is cooked in two huge cauldrons and served to pilgrims.

Around the world

In Islamic countries, the major festivals are public holidays. Elsewhere, Muslims take time off work to celebrate. In some countries, other special Muslim festivals take place, such as Sufi celebrations commemorating the lives of great holy men and women of the past, or saints.

A drummer at a Muslim festival in Tunisia.

East and Southeast Asia

Islam was taken to Southeast Asia by sailors crossing the Indian Ocean in search of trade. Other merchants took the land route, following the ancient Silk Road through central Asia to the Chinese capital of Chang'an. Along the islands and shores of Indonesia and Malaysia, Muslim traders established strategic ports that developed into flourishing city-states. Today, Indonesia has a greater Muslim population than any other country in the world, while Malaysia has a Muslim majority and China has an important minority of 38 million Muslims.

A mosque in Kuala Kangsar, Malaysia.

An Islamic tombstone in Indrapuri, Sumatra.

Across the Indian Ocean

The southern mainland of present-day Malaysia and the coasts of the Indonesian islands were important stopping places on the sea route from Arabia and India to China and the Far East. As early as the 11th century, Muslim traders sailed across the Indian Ocean to the South China Sea. They passed through the Strait of Malacca, between Sumatra and Malaysia, and at ports on the strait traded their goods for Indonesian spices and sweet-smelling woods, as well as Malayan gold.

A ship sailing through the Strait of Malacca.

Malacca

The city port of Malacca (or Melaka), on the south-west coast of the Malay peninsula, was founded around 1400. Its first ruler, a Sumatran prince named Paramesvara (ruled 1403–24), became a Muslim in 1414 and took the title Sultan Iskandar Shah. By the late 15th century, Malacca attracted 15,000 merchants from all parts of Asia, including Arabs, Indians, and Chinese. Thai forces were defeated in 1456, but this important city finally fell to the Portuguese in 1511. They held Malacca until 1641, when it was captured by the Dutch.

Left: This miniature shows a Muslim prince of the "Eastern Isles".

Right: View of Malacca.

Samudra

From 1295, the region of Samudra (on the northern coast of Sumatra) became an important center for the spread of Islam. At that time, there were two small trading settlements at the ports of Pasai and Perlak, which came to be ruled by Muslim kings. By the end of the 14th century, Pasai was a rich city, and the ruling Muslims commanded the loyalty of the local people. Samudra was an excellent stretch of coast for sailing ships to shelter in, well away from the pirate lairs at the southern end of the strait.

Right: The maritime compass, invented in China, was brought to the west by Arab traders in the 13th century.

Aceh

Founded around 1525, Aceh took over as the leading harbor kingdom in Sumatra. It reached its height under Sultan Iskandar Muda (ruled 1607–36), who in a series of naval actions gained control over Malaysian ports such as Perak, which gave him access to tin. The sultan encouraged Islamic scholars and Sufi mystics and made Aceh a center of learning. He also allied himself with the Mughals of India and the Turkish Ottomans.

Sufi missionaries

Many different Sufi orders helped to spread Islam eastward. One such brotherhood is the Qadiriyya order, which was originally founded in Baghdad. In 1644, a young man named Yusuf from the island of Celebes, who was sailing for Arabia, made port at Aceh and joined the Qadiriyya brotherhood there. He then spent 25 years in the Middle East studying other Sufi orders, and on his return helped the Javanese in their resistance to Dutch rule. Today, many pilgrims visit the tomb of Yusuf of Makasar (1626–99) in Celebes (modern Sulawesi).

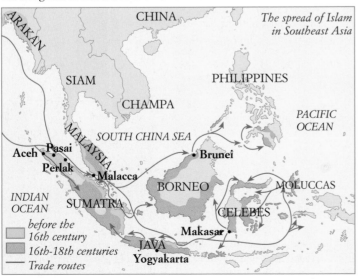

The spread of Islam in Southeast Asia

CHINA
ARAKAN
SIAM
CHAMPA
PHILIPPINES
PACIFIC OCEAN
SOUTH CHINA SEA
MALAYSIA
Aceh • Pasai
Perlak •
• Malacca
• Brunei
BORNEO
MOLUCCAS
INDIAN OCEAN
SUMATRA
CELEBES
Makasar •
JAVA
Yogyakarta

before the 16th century
16th-18th centuries
Trade routes

Using the monsoon winds

For Muslim merchants, the Malay peninsula and Indonesian archipelago were a rich source of gold, tin, pepper, and other spices. Beyond lay China, with its silk, porcelain, and other luxury goods. Sea travel from Arabia and India along the so-called Spice Route was made easier by the powerful monsoon winds. These blow from the southwest from April to October, powering sailing ships toward China, and blow the other way for the rest of the year, helping merchants back across the Indian Ocean.

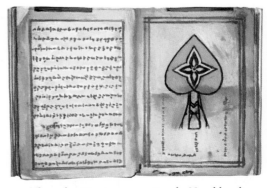

These short tracts were written by Naqshbandiyya members on the island of Celebes, Indonesia, in 1759.

Java

The oldest Muslim tombstone in Java is dated 1082, but it was another 400 years before Islam had a serious presence on the island. In 1478, the Hindu kingdom of Majahapit was taken over by an Islamic conquest, but separate regional courts and customs remained. Under Sultan Agung (ruled 1613–46), the Muslim state of Mataram dominated most of Java. Agung began building a mosque in Yogyakarta, but it was not completed until the late 18th century.

Left: Posters like this are bought by pilgrims visiting the tombs of the nine wali (saints or holy men) who are thought to have first brought the message of Islam to Java.

Left: This traditional Javanese shadow puppet represents Sunan Bonang, one of the nine wali.

Right: Pages from the Serat Ambiya, a collection of stories that mixes ancient Javanese and Islamic traditions.

War against the Dutch

The Java War of 1825–30 is known to Indonesians as Dipo Negoro's War. Prince Dipo Negoro (1785–1855) was the son of the sultan of Yogyakarta, an Islamic state that was created in 1755 by treaty with the ruling Dutch. In 1825, the prince led a rebellion against Dutch officials in what many Muslims saw as a "holy war." For three years, his guerrilla tactics were successful, but he was finally captured by the Dutch and sent into exile in Celebes.

Left: Prince Dipo Negoro.

Reform movements

In the early 20th century, a number of Islamic reform movements appeared in Indonesia. They worked toward Islamic unity and social equality. One of the largest groups is the Muhammadiyah, founded in Yogyakarta in 1912. Since then, the number of Indonesians making a pilgrimage to Mecca has increased enormously, and many have returned with a stronger sense of Arabian Islam.

Right: Some hajj pilgrims adopt a more Arabian style of clothing when they return from Mecca.

Pre-Islamic traditions

Through the centuries, Muslims in southeast Asia have had to adapt to pre-Islamic traditions, including pagan customs. When Islam arrived, many islands already had strong Hindu or Buddhist communities. In many cases, rulers and the important merchant classes were Muslim, while their subjects and others retained their traditional way of life. In Malaysia today, where more than half the population are Muslim, there are strong Buddhist, Hindu, and Christian minorities.

Above: Carved wooden panel in the Great Mosque at Xian.

Routes to China

Apart from those traders who reached southern China through the Strait of Malacca, most went by land along the famous routes later known collectively as the Silk Road. This had existed since ancient times, leading all the way from the Middle East to the old capital of China, Chang'an (present-day Xian). The route passed through Baghdad, Samarkand, and Kashgar, skirting the Taklimakan Desert on the way to eastern China. From the 7th century, caravans of Muslim traders carried wool, linen, ivory, amber, and many other goods with them, along with their firm belief in Islam. The first mosque was built in Chang'an in 742.

Above: A 16th-century porcelain bowl made in eastern China with a Persian inscription.

The Hui

The merchants, craftworkers, soldiers, and scholars who came to China from the Middle East and Central Asia came to be known as the Hui people (also called the Tonggan). Today, Muslims are mostly concentrated in the western provinces of China, especially Xinjiang, and many are farmers. Down the centuries, several other Chinese groups have also turned to Islam, many of them influenced by Sufism, which made a great impact from the 17th century onward.

Left: Entrance to a Chinese mosque.

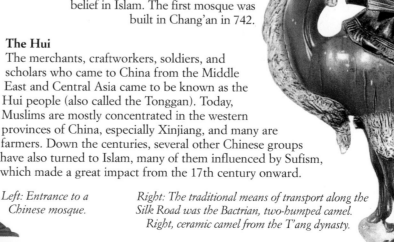

Right: The traditional means of transport along the Silk Road was the Bactrian, two-humped camel. Right, ceramic camel from the T'ang dynasty.

Women in Islam

In Muslim societies of the past, the view of a woman's role was mainly as a wife, mother, and homemaker. This meant that girls received very little formal education and took no real part in the wider affairs of their country. The situation began to change in the 20th century, however, as women throughout the world strove for equal rights. In recent years, many young Muslim women have decided to devote more time to their education and career before getting married and having children. Some have chosen to discard their veils and wear more modern dress, while at the same time retaining their total commitment to Islam.

Above: A Persian miniature of a maid dressing her wealthy mistress's hair.

Women's role

The Qur'an teaches that men and women are equal in the eyes of Allah, and that women are always to be respected and protected. While men are responsible for providing for their families, women are expected to control affairs within the home. Muslim women have always been allowed to inherit and own property in their own right, which gave them a distinct advantage over women of other cultures in past centuries.

Above: This Swahili bride's arms and legs have been decorated with henna before her wedding.

Right: A husband and wife accuse each other before a judge.

Below: Bedouins are Muslim nomads who live in the Arabian and Sahara deserts. This Bedouin woman is spinning wool in the women's quarters of her family's large tent. The daughter will learn her mother's skills at a young age.

Marriage

In Islam, marriage is seen as a legal contract rather than a religious sacrament. Women traditionally marry young and can have only one Muslim husband, though in theory they might have to share him with up to three other women. In most Muslim societies, however, men have only one wife – in many countries this is the law. Any dowry agreed in the marriage contract is paid to the bride rather than her father, and it is hers to keep if she is later divorced. Arranged marriages still exist in more traditional societies, but a marriage must be with the consent of both partners.

This Eritrean Rashaida man certainly believes in polygamy (marrying more than one woman). He is leading his three wives to a festival.

Divorce

Islam permits married people to get divorced. Divorce laws and customs vary from country to country, but there are generally no lengthy legalities. If a man wants to divorce his wife, he must announce his intention three times and then wait for three months. If the woman is expecting a baby, the husband must wait nine months. A woman may divorce her husband if he refuses to look after her or ill-treats her. A divorced woman may remarry as soon as she wants to.

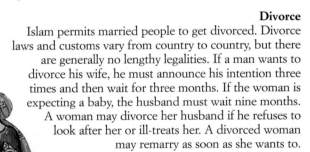

Below: Celebrations for the birth of a son to one of the wives of Mughal emperor Akbar the Great, in 1569.

Family life

Muslims believe that the family is the basis of society, and most have a large circle of relatives to whom they feel very close. Muslim wives are traditionally respected for having children, especially for producing male heirs. In turn, children are brought up to respect and obey their mothers. Today, many Muslims agree that it is reasonable for married couples to plan their family by using birth control.

Right: At a private wedding party, some female guests have removed their veils.

Left: Some women continue to cover themselves completely. This Afghan woman is wearing a burka.

Traditional and modern dress

According to the Qur'an, women should always dress modestly. They are not specifically told to cover themselves completely, and the tradition of the *hijab*, or veil, came originally from the Byzantines. In some Islamic countries, it is customary for women to wear cloaklike garments, called *chadors*, which leave only the face free, or *burkas*, which have a grill in front of the eyes so that women can see without being seen. In recent years, many Muslim women have started to wear modern versions of traditional styles, with headscarves and long sleeves.

Religious duties

Muslim women take their religious duties as seriously as men. Many women, and especially those with young children, find it easier to pray at home rather than in a mosque. When they do worship at the mosque, women usually form rows behind the men or in a separate area. Women fast in the same way as men, though they are not expected to do so fully if they are pregnant, have very young babies, or are unwell. In recent times it has become more usual for women to make a pilgrimage to Mecca.

Left: An Ottoman Turkish woman on a pilgrimage to Mecca.

Right: In this 17th-century illustration, musicians and dancers entertain women in the harem.

Right: This Persian illustration shows women sitting in a separate area of the mosque during a religious service.

The harem

The word *harem* comes from Arabic *haram* ("forbidden"). It came to mean the sanctuary of the women's quarters that was forbidden to others, apart from the male head of the household and his sons and brothers. Historically, there were harems in many royal palaces, where the ruler's wives and mistresses, plus their female relatives and servants, lived. They appear in many legendary stories.

At work

Though women are allowed to work, most Muslims believe that they should not be forced to. In the modern world, however, more and more young women have to go out to work to support their family. This can create problems for mothers if day-care for their children is not available. Many of those without good qualifications take domestic jobs or work in factories. In the workplace, Muslim women have the right to be treated equally and with respect.

A seamstress in Oman.

Below: These girls attend a university in Algeria.

Below: Benazir Bhutto became prime minister of Pakistan at the age of 35.

Education

Until recent times, there was little education for girls in the Islamic world. They stayed at home and learned domestic duties from their mothers. Today, most countries have full-time education for both boys and girls. Girls also follow Islamic studies and learn Arabic at their mosque school. Many go on to university, to become as well-educated and qualified as their brothers.

Politics

During the 20th century, Muslim women began to take an active part in politics, as their countries gradually gave them the right to vote and represent others. In the 1920s, the Egyptian feminist Huda Sharawi led demonstrations and attended international conferences. In 1988, Benazir Bhutto was elected prime minister of Pakistan, to become the first female leader of a Muslim country. She was soon followed by Khaleda Zia in Bangladesh and Tansu Ciller in Turkey.

The emergence of Muslim states

By the end of the 18th century, the important powers of the Muslim world had grown weak. Safavid rule in Persia had collapsed, the Mughals had lost power in India, and even the great Ottoman Empire was in decline. This allowed European countries the opportunity to colonize many Muslim regions. From early in the 20th century, however, the countries of northern Africa, the Middle East, and southern Asia began reclaiming their independence. They went on to form the modern Islamic states that we know today.

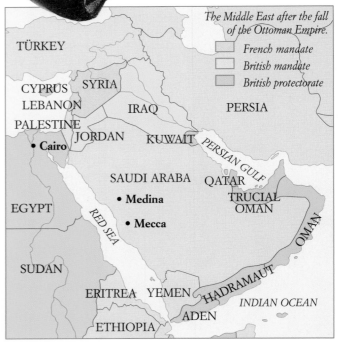

The Arab revolt
During the First World War, Britain helped the Arabs rebel against the Ottomans, promising that an Arab government would rule over the former Ottoman lands after the war. The commander of the Arab revolt, Emir Faisal, succeeded in capturing Damascus in 1918. Despite this and the previous promises, the League of Nations decided to divide the Arab lands that had been held by the Ottomans between Britain and France.

Emir Faisal (1885–1933) became King of Syria in 1920 but was expelled by the French. The following year, he became King of Iraq, which was under British control.

The birth of Turkey
After the First World War, the Ottoman sultan was deposed, and in 1923 the new Republic of Turkey was declared. Its first president was Mustafa Kemal (1881–1938), who later took the name Atatürk, meaning "father of the Turks." The new republic rejected much of traditional Islamic culture, changing the system of law and replacing Arabic with the Roman alphabet.

Left: This poster shows Atatürk's horse led by an unveiled young woman, who represents the new Republic of Turkey.

The Middle East after the fall of the Ottoman Empire.
- French mandate
- British mandate
- British protectorate

TÜRKEY
CYPRUS
SYRIA
LEBANON
IRAQ
PALESTINE
JORDAN
KUWAIT
• Cairo
SAUDI ARABA
QATAR
TRUCIAL OMAN
EGYPT
• Medina
• Mecca
PERSIA
PERSIAN GULF
OMAN
RED SEA
SUDAN
ERITREA YEMEN HADRAMAUT
ADEN INDIAN OCEAN
ETHIOPIA

Saudi Arabia
In 1902, Abd al-Aziz ibn Saud (1880–1953) captured Riyadh – in previous centuries the Saud dynasty had ruled a region near modern Riyadh but had been forced to flee to Kuwait. He then went on to take other regions of the peninsula. In 1925, he captured Hejaz, which included the holy cities of Mecca and Medina. Ibn Saud then united the Arabian regions and, in 1932, named the union after his family and proclaimed the Kingdom of Saudi Arabia.

The Saudi emblem on the wall of King Faisal's modern Specialist Hospital in Riyadh, the capital of Saudi Arabia.

The mandate system
The League of Nations called the lands supervised by Britain and France after 1920 "mandated territories" (see the map, above). Britain had the mandate (that is, order or commission) to supervise Palestine and Mesopotamia, which was later renamed Iraq, while France was given the mandate over Syria. Part of Palestine became Transjordan (later renamed Jordan) and part of Syria became Lebanon. These divisions weakened the Arab countries even further, but by 1946 Iraq, Jordan, Lebanon, and Syria had all achieved independence.

Egypt
The British occupied Egypt in 1882 after putting down an Arab revolt against the Ottomans. After becoming a British protectorate, Egypt gained independence in 1922 under King Fuad. In 1945, Egypt became a founder member of both the United Nations and the Arab League. Seven years later, Gamal Abdel Nasser (1918–70) led a group of army officers in overthrowing the monarchy, and British forces left the Republic of Egypt in 1954.

Above: The first ships passed through the Suez Canal in 1869. The canal runs through Egypt to connect the Mediterranean and Red Seas, saving ships thousands of miles between Asia and Europe.

Right: President Nasser, who, in 1956, nationalized the Suez Canal. He was seen as a leader of the Arab world.

Discovering oil
The Persian Gulf states' interest in oil began in 1911, when a British company discovered the "black gold" in Iran. In 1932, an American company struck oil in Bahrain, and six years later in Saudi Arabia. During the 1950s, the Gulf states began taking some control of foreign oil firms, and in 1960 Saudi Arabia, Iran, Iraq, and Kuwait became founder members of the Organization of Petroleum Exporting Countries (OPEC). Oil soon brought wealth and many changes to the region, and Saudi Arabia is still the world's top oil producer.

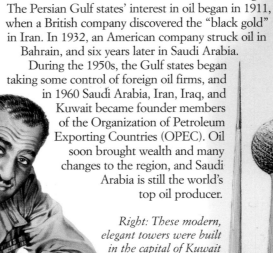

Right: These modern, elegant towers were built in the capital of Kuwait in 1977. Building projects such as these were funded by wealth from oil.

Palestine

In 1917, Britain promised to help establish a Jewish homeland in Palestine, which they later controlled as a mandated territory. This declaration followed the establishment of the Zionist movement twenty years earlier. Jewish immigration to Palestine increased, especially after the Nazis came to power in Germany in the 1930s, and this caused an Arab revolt. In 1947, the United Nations voted to divide Palestine into an Arab state and a Jewish state. This division was not accepted by the Arabs, however.

Zionist leaders are portrayed with their aims – land to farm and the Western Wall in Jerusalem at which to pray.

Foundation of Israel

After the British mandate in Palestine ended, the new Jewish state of Israel was proclaimed in 1948. Arabs from surrounding lands immediately attacked the new state, claiming that it stood on their Palestinian territory. Israeli forces drove the Arabs back and gained most of Palestine. The region of the West Bank (of the River Jordan) fell to Jordan, and Egypt occupied the Gaza Strip, along the Mediterranean coast.

Right: Many Palestinian Arabs were forced to leave Israel and live in refugee camps or settle in neighboring Muslim countries.

Iran

From 1794 to 1925, Persia was a kingdom ruled over by shahs of the Qajar dynasty. It was independent but greatly influenced by other powers such as Britain and Russia. A revolt led to the army officer Reza being made shah in 1925, and ten years later the country's name was officially changed to Iran. Reza was succeeded by his son, Mohammed Reza Pahlavi (1918–80), who ruled as Shah of Iran from 1941. In 1979, a revolution overthrew the shah and declared Iran an Islamic republic.

Fath Ali (1797–1834) was the last Persian shah to rule without European interference.

Right: In 1936, Iranian women were banned from wearing veils and had to adopt Western clothes.

Above: Before civil war broke out, the Lebanese promoted their capital as a wonderful Mediterranean city.

War in the Middle East

Further Arab-Israeli wars broke out in 1956, 1967, and 1973. In Lebanon, which became independent in 1943, there was constant tension between Muslim and Christian groups. Civil war finally broke out there in 1975 and lasted for over a year. There were also wars in North Yemen (1962–70) and Sudan, which had become independent in 1956.

Algeria

The French first invaded Algeria in 1830. After the Second World War, a struggle for independence began. In 1954, the Algerian National Liberation Front (FLN) took up the armed struggle, which lasted until independence in 1962. Just three years later the new republic's government was overthrown by a revolutionary council.

Right: Algerian independence is announced with the Islamic star and crescent.

Building started in 1966 on the vast King Faisal Mosque in Islamabad, the capital of Pakistan.

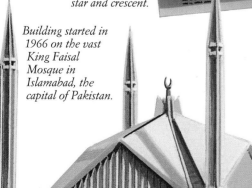

Pakistan and Bangladesh

The Muslim League was formed in India in 1906. When India was coming close to becoming independent in 1940, the League pressed for a separate Muslim state. To achieve this, Pakistan was founded as two regions in 1947, and twenty-five years later the Muslim Bengalis of East Pakistan achieved their own independence as Bangladesh.

Mohammed Ali Jinnah (1876–1948), president of the Muslim League, helped create Pakistan and was its first governor-general.

This poster of 1945 shows Sukarno and his future vice president Mohammed Hatta. It reads "Independence!"

Indonesia

The Indonesian islands were a Dutch colony from 1798 to 1945, when a revolutionary government was set up by Achmad Sukarno (1901–70). Full independence came in 1949, and Sukarno became the republic of Indonesia's first president. Today, Indonesia has the greatest number of Muslims of any country in the world.

Islamism

There is growing support in the Muslim world for Islamism, or Islamic fundamentalism. This movement has come about as an attempt to provide a cultural and political alternative to modern nonreligious governments. The Islamist movements began many years ago in response to Western colonial influence and the decline of the Muslim world. Since then the idea of Islamic revival has spread, as many Muslims support an increase of Islamic values and a stricter application of Islamic laws. In recent years, some Islamist groups in both Muslim and non-Muslim regions of the world have reacted to failure to achieve their ends by turning to violence. This has only served to heighten fear and distrust of Islam among non-Muslims.

In 1979 President Sadat of Egypt (right) reached a peace agreement with Israel's prime minister Menachem Begin (left). Here they celebrate the agreement with U.S. President Jimmy Carter.

The Iranian Revolution

In 1979, the religious leader Ayatollah Ruholla Khomeini (1902–89) returned from 16 years of exile to lead the revolution that overthrew the Shah of Iran. The Ayatollah (an Arabic word meaning "token of God") ruled the country by strict Islamic laws and tried to get rid of all Western, non-Muslim influences. He called on all Muslims to rise up against "oppressive, non-Islamic" governments. From 1980 to 1988, his country was at war with Iraq over disputed territory.

Left: In this revolutionary poster, Ayatollah Khomeini stands over the defeated shah, who is hanging on to the coat-tails of Uncle Sam (America).

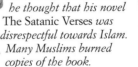

In 1989 Ayatollah Khomeini condemned Salman Rushdie because he thought that his novel The Satanic Verses was disrespectful towards Islam. Many Muslims burned copies of the book.

The Muslim Brotherhood

The Islamist group called the Muslim Brotherhood was founded in 1928 by the Egyptian schoolteacher Hasan al-Banna (1906–49). In the 1940s, it posed a threat to the Egyptian monarchy and in 1954 was suppressed after a failed attempt to assassinate President Nasser. In the 1970s, the Brotherhood was revived, and in 1981 extremists linked to the organization killed Nasser's successor Anwar Sadat (1918–81).

These Sudanese women belong to an Islamist army unit.

Sudan

Since independence in 1956, there has been civil war in Sudan between the ruling Muslims of the north and the animists and Christians of the south. In 1983, President Nimeiri established Islamic law in Sudan, but two years later he was forced from power. Since 1989 the government has been influenced by the NIF (National Islamic Front), a fundamentalist political group founded by Hasan al-Turabi. Civil war and famine have claimed about 1.5 million lives in the past twenty years. Today, about 70 percent of Sudanese are Muslims.

Afghanistan

From 1979 to 1989 Muslim Afghan guerrillas, called Mujahedin, fought against their government and the Soviet Russian forces that supported it. After the Soviets withdrew, the Mujahedin proclaimed an Islamic state in 1992, but fighting continued between rival groups. Four years later, the capital of Kabul was seized by forces of the Taliban, a hard-line Islamist group, which imposed strict laws. They stopped women from working and their daughters from going to school, and banned music, TV, and movies.

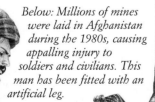

Below: Millions of mines were laid in Afghanistan during the 1980s, causing appalling injury to soldiers and civilians. This man has been fitted with an artificial leg.

Pakistan

Pakistan became an Islamic Republic in 1956, nine years after it came into being. This led to stricter Islamic laws being imposed. During the 1980s and 1990s, the Pakistan government was plagued by corruption. Prime Minister Benazir Bhutto (see page 51) was twice dismissed, and the military under General Pervez Musharraf took power in 1999. During this whole period there has been continued disagreement and struggle with India over the mountainous border region of Kashmir.

The Badshahi Mosque, in Pakistan's second largest city of Lahore. The mosque was built in 1674 by the Mughals.

Above: In 2001 the Taliban destroyed this and other statues of the Buddha in Afghanistan, saying that they led to forbidden idol worship.

Knowledge and welfare

Many Islamists are deeply concerned about the gap between rich and poor people throughout the world. They refer to the duty of all Muslims to give charitably to those who are less fortunate than themselves and believe that non-Muslim governments in the West should also take more responsibility for the poor. As well as promoting Qur'anic classes, Islamist organizations publish a great deal of material on the meaning and importance of Islam and a strict Muslim way of life.

Islamist pamphlets are published all over the world.

A doctor working for the Palestinian Red Crescent holds a young patient. This medical organization is part of the International Federation of the Red Cross and Red Crescent.

Self-proclaimed islamic Republic

Extent of Islam

Political parties

Many Islamist scholars believe that an ideal Islamic society would be based on a system of consultation between political leaders and the people. In reality, many Islamic states have become forms of dictatorship, where ordinary citizens have little say. Attempts have been made in some Muslim countries to include Islamists in elected, democratic governments. In the Hashemite Kingdom of Jordan, for example, the Arab National Union was the only political organization allowed in the 1970s. By 1993, however, Jordanian politics included the Islamic Action Party.

A Lebanese sheikh preaches support for Hezbollah in a Beirut mosque.

Philippines

Islamist groups are active all over the world, including the Far East. In the Philippines, Muslims make up 5 percent of the population, while the vast majority is Christian. In 1968, a group known as the Moro National Liberation Front (MNLF) was set up to represent the Muslim Moro people of the southern Philippines and demand a separate homeland for them. Many thousands of people have been killed in the struggle, and in 1996 the Muslim rebels were offered peace and their own autonomous region.

Left: King Hussein ruled Jordan from 1953 to 1999. On his death he was succeeded by his son Abdullah II.

Right: Osama bin Laden was the main target of American antiterrorist forces after the destruction of New York's World Trade Center in 2001.

Below: Women mourn the death of a young soldier in Algeria. Violence erupted there when the military stopped The Islamic Salvation Front (FIS) from taking power after elections in 1991.

Al-Qaida

The terrorist support group called al-Qaida (meaning "the base") is thought to have been founded around 1989. Osama bin Laden and others led groups of Arab volunteers who fought the Soviets in Afghanistan. They were based first in Sudan, and then in Afghanistan, where they had close links with the Taliban. Al-Qaida and Bin Laden were held responsible for the attacks on New York and Washington on September 11, 2001. This led to a worldwide campaign by America and its allies to destroy the al-Qaida network.

Extremist groups

Many extremist Islamic organizations grew out of specific events or problems within the Muslim world. In the Middle East, some were stimulated by the revolution in Iran and the continuing Arab-Israeli conflict. The extremist Shi'ite group Hezbollah (meaning "party of God") became active in Lebanon in the late 1980s. It was held responsible for hijackings and hostage-taking before making attacks on Israel in 1996. Several other groups have also taken to violence and terrorism.

55

Consecration

On their pilgrimage, Muslims must enter a state of *ihram*, which means "consecration." This helps them to concentrate totally on their sacred tasks and includes wearing special clothes. Male pilgrims put on two simple pieces of white cloth (see left), while women wear a plain, full-length dress, leaving their face and hands bare. Everyone must go barefoot or wear sandals. During the hajj, pilgrims must not wear perfume, cut their hair or fingernails, or have sexual relations.

Pre-Islamic origins

A tradition of annual fairs grew up in ancient Mecca, and the oasis town was already a place of pilgrimage in pre-Islamic times. Special rocks and stones were worshiped, and this included the Black Stone in the Kaaba shrine, which is probably a meteorite. The cubic shrine itself is also very old and was mentioned in the writings of Sicilian Greek historian Diodorus Siculus around 60 BCE.

This miniature shows Meccans surrounding the ancient Kaaba shrine.

The Hajj

Every Muslim who is able to, must make a special pilgrimage to the center of the Islamic world – Mecca. This pilgrimage, called the hajj, is made between the 8th and 13th of the month of Dhu'l-Hijjah, the last in the Islamic calendar. A pilgrimage at any other time, or one that does not include all the key elements, does not have the same significance. The hajj is one of the five Pillars of Islam (see page 12), but the Qur'an makes it clear that Muslims should only make the pilgrimage if they are healthy and can afford to provide for the families they leave behind. Sometimes a family is able to send just one member to represent everyone, and for those who cannot go it is the genuine intention to do so that counts.

Left: This 13th-century illustration shows medieval pilgrims traveling together in a caravan.

Above: Mount Arafat, as shown in an 18th-century pilgrims' guide.

Circling the Kaaba

On arrival in Mecca, pilgrims hurry to the courtyard of the Great Mosque. There they perform the *tawaf*, which means circling the Kaaba seven times in an counterclockwise direction. If possible, they run for the first three circuits. They also try to kiss or touch the Black Stone as they pass, or otherwise raise a hand in salute. Old people and invalids are carried around.

Above: The Kaaba shrine has a cover of black silk and cotton embroidered with verses from the Qur'an in gold thread.

Traveling to Mecca

Years ago Muslims walked most of the way to Mecca, and those from faraway lands took months to get there. Today, most pilgrims arrive at the King Abdul Aziz Airport in Jedda, on the Red Sea coast, before taking a bus for the 44-mile journey to Mecca. Some pilgrims choose to walk from Jedda to Mecca. All are organized into groups led by experienced guides. Only Muslims can enter Mecca at this time. More than two million pilgrims make the journey each year.

The Mount of Mercy

On the ninth day of the month, pilgrims gather on the plain that leads to Arafat, the Mount of Mercy. This is where Muslims believe Allah reunited Adam and Eve, and where the Prophet Muhammad gave his final sermon. Pilgrims stay there from noon to sunset, praying and worshiping Allah. This important part of hajj is called *wuquf* ("standing"), because pilgrims make their stand before God.

Left: Pilgrims pray and meditate on hills beside the plain of Arafat.

Below: Today, many pilgrims choose to take a crowded bus to the plain of Arafat.

Mountain of Mercy

Mina

Arafat

Muzfalidah

Great Mosque

tents

The Feast of Sacrifice

On the tenth day of the month, pilgrims who can afford it must sacrifice an animal such as a sheep or a goat. This commemorates the sacrifice that Ibrahim was prepared to make by killing his own son, before Allah stopped him and a ram was sacrificed instead. Today, many pilgrims buy coupons that correspond to animals killed in a slaughterhouse. Some of the meat is given to the poor, and the rest is frozen for later use.

After the Feast of Sacrifice, pilgrims have their head shaved or their hair clipped, and women cut off a symbolic lock.

Stoning the pillars

From the plain of Arafat, pilgrims head back to Muzdalifah, where they say special prayers and pick up small pebbles from the ground. Then they continue on to Mina, where there are three stopping places with stone pillars called *jamras*. The pillars represent the place where Ibrahim and Ismail were tempted by Satan to disobey God and threw stones to drive him away. The pilgrims throw their pebbles at the pillars, showing that they too will do everything to drive the devil away.

The Black Stone

Muslims believe that the Kaaba was first built by Adam. It was later rebuilt by Ibrahim, who received the Black Stone from the angel Jibril and placed it inside the shrine. In 605, after the Kaaba was damaged by floods, Meccan leaders argued over who would replace the stone. Asked to decide, Muhammad allowed the tribal leaders to carry the stone together on a blanket. He then put the stone in position himself, and everyone was happy.

Left: Muhammad lifts the Black Stone from the blanket held by the leaders of Mecca.

Above: Overhead view of pilgrims stoning a jamra *pillar.*

Completing the pilgrimage

At the end of the hajj, pilgrims circle the Kaaba again, just as they did at the start. This final *tawaf* completes the pilgrimage. A male pilgrim is then known as a hajji, and a woman is called a hajjah. While they are in Saudi Arabia, many Muslims take the opportunity to visit other important sites, such as the Prophet's tomb in Medina.

Finding water

Two further rituals commemorate the desperate search for water by Ismael's mother, Hagar. Pilgrims run or walk seven times between two small hills near the Kaaba, just as Hagar did. Today the hills are joined by a special passageway. Pilgrims also drink from the Zamzam well in the courtyard of the Great Mosque. It marks the place where, according to tradition, baby Ismael dug his heels into the sand and a spring of water burst out to save his life and that of his mother.

Right: Some pilgrims take water from the Zamzam well home with them, to share with others.

Above: This 12th-century certificate states that a pilgrim made the long journey to Mecca.

Right: Some pilgrims celebrate their return from hajj through paintings on the outside walls of their homes.

All over the world

As the map (left) shows, Islam is a global religion, with significant numbers of Muslims in most regions of the world. Islam began in Arabia, and still today the people of the Arabian peninsula are mainly Muslim – only 5 percent of Arabs are non-Muslims. Yet, overall, today's Arabs account for just 20 percent of the world's Muslims, who represent the majority religion in forty-seven countries. Indonesia has the greatest number of Muslims (181 million), followed by Pakistan (141 million), and India (124 million, but forming just 12 percent of the population, which is mainly Hindu). Thirty percent of the world's Muslims live in Africa.

Above: Malcolm X gave up his family name because he said it was given to his ancestors by slave owners. Many black Americans converted to Islam as a way of rediscovering an African identity.

Islam today

Right: The Islamic Center in New York is a focal point for the city's international community of Muslims.

Muslims strongly believe that their world stretches beyond national boundaries. The Arabic term *umma*, meaning "people," refers to the whole community of Muslims everywhere, who are bound together by their faith. Since Islam is the fastest growing religion, this community is getting bigger. In many parts of the world, Muslims live happily and peacefully with their non-Muslim neighbors, but there are trouble spots where distrust and fear continually lead to violence. Muslims believe that Islam will help them meet the challenges of the 21st century.

In the Americas

There are significant numbers of Muslims in the South American countries of Guyana and Surinam. More than 6 million Muslims live in the United States, where most are immigrants from all over the world who arrived in the second half of the 20th century. Up to a third of U.S. Muslims are African Americans who have converted since the 1960s. Many belong to the Nation of Islam movement, which supports black liberation. The movement, founded in 1930, has had famous leaders in Elijah Muhammad (1897–1975) and Malcolm X (1925–65). Since 1978, Louis Farrakhan has led a "black pride" group.

Demonstrators hold up their message in Algiers.

A Muslim fast-food restaurant in England. Muslims have set up shops and restaurants to offer food that is prepared in an Islamic way.

Modern way of life

Many Islamists (see pages 54–55) support a return to a stricter implementation of Islamic law. Others believe that this would not fit in well with the modern world, especially for Muslims living in non-Islamic countries. Some Islamic scholars feel that there is a lack of understanding of modern science and technology, despite the fact that centuries ago Muslims were at the forefront in these areas. These are issues that most Muslims wish to resolve in the 21st century.

Below: Acting as a link between the ancient and modern worlds, a Bedouin carries one means of transport in another.

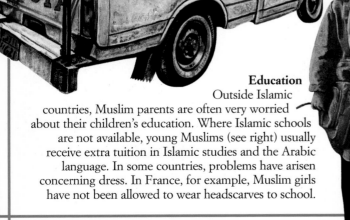

Western Europe

Though they represent a small proportion of the total population (from 2 to 5 percent), there are many Muslims in countries such as France, Germany, and the United Kingdom. Many emigrated from former colonies – North Africa to France, the Commonwealth to Britain – in the second half of the 20th century, mostly to seek work. In some cases, they were welcomed as temporary guest workers, who then found it difficult to gain full citizenship. The biggest challenge for European Muslims is to fit in with a predominantly Christian or nonreligious society, while at the same time keeping their identity and upholding their Islamic values.

Education

Outside Islamic countries, Muslim parents are often very worried about their children's education. Where Islamic schools are not available, young Muslims (see right) usually receive extra tuition in Islamic studies and the Arabic language. In some countries, problems have arisen concerning dress. In France, for example, Muslim girls have not been allowed to wear headscarves to school.

Uzbek Muslims at their local mosque.

Religious revival

During the 1990s, many people in former Soviet republics that had gained independence began practicing Islam openly again. Russia itself has a Muslim minority of 12 million people, and Uzbekistan has 22 million.

Some Uzbeks practice Sufism, while the radically political Islamic Party of Turkistan has vowed to install Islamic regimes in Uzbekistan and neighboring countries. Islam is the majority religion in Azerbaijan, Kazakhstan (47 percent Muslim, 44 percent Orthodox Christian), Kyrgyzstan, Tajikistan, and Turkmenistan, where altogether 29 million Muslims live.

This girl is putting money into her family's charity box.

Saudi Arabia

The land of Muhammad's birth has become a rich country because of its oil fields, including the world's largest at Ghawar, which produces several million barrels of oil every day. The country is governed by a wealthy monarchy, which imposes a strict form of Islam called Wahhabism. In the 1990s, Saudi wealth suffered slightly due to falling oil prices.

Helping others

It is an Islamic duty to give charitably to the poor (see page 12), and there are many Muslim organizations that raise funds to help the world's poorest people. One such nongovernmental organization, Islamic Relief, was set up in the United Kingdom in 1984 and now has fund-raising offices throughout Europe and America.

Left: The governor of the Saudi capital, Riyadh, listens to a request made by a citizen. Such audiences by leaders and officials are traditional in the region.

Global organizations

The Organization of the Islamic Conference (OIC) was founded in 1969, in Morocco. It is made up of 56 country members, with headquarters in Jeddah, Saudi Arabia. Its aim is to defend the interests and ensure the progress and well-being of Muslims everywhere. The Muslim World League, or Rabita, was founded in 1962 and is based in Mecca. As a nongovernmental organization, it has observer status at the United Nations.

Left: A young Palestinian refugee shows her picture of Jerusalem.

Right: Nusrat Fateh Ali Khan, world famous singer of qawwali, the Muslim devotional music of Sufis in Pakistan. After his recent death his nephew Rahat carries on his legacy.

Art and culture

Many of today's mosques and other Islamic buildings are based on traditional designs but have clearly been influenced by modern trends. Domes and minarets are often designed to fit in with their surroundings. The ancient art of Islamic calligraphy is kept alive by modern graphic artists (see above). In music, traditional styles are passed on from generation to generation.

Below: The Martyrs' Monument in Baghdad, Iraq, was built in 1983 on an island in the middle of a lake. It is made up of two halves of a huge dome covered with blue tiles.

Palestine

The Palestinian *intifada*, or uprising, against Israeli occupation of the West Bank began in 1987. Though further peace agreements were signed between Israel and the Palestinian Arabs in the 1990s, violence broke out again at the turn of the millennium. The Palestinians continue to call for the right of millions of refugees to return to their homeland, which the Israelis claim as their territory. In 2002, Yassir Arafat, leader of the Palestine Liberation Organization (right), was besieged by the Israelis for several weeks in his headquarters in the West Bank. The problem of Palestine remains unsolved.

Index